New Pathways
a dialogue in Christian Higher Education

Essays in honor of
Raleigh Kirby Godsey
on the occasion of his inauguration as
the seventeenth president of
Mercer University

New Pathways

a dialogue in
Christian Higher Education

Edited by
Ben C. Fisher

Mercer University Press
Macon, Georgia

New Pathways: a dialogue in Christian Higher Education

Library of Congress Card Number 80-80255

ISBN 086554-000-4

Dedicated to
Christian unity, knowledge and freedom

Foreword

New beginnings afford educational institutions the opportunity to re-evaluate their *raison d'être*. This initial volume from the Mercer University Press is occasioned by a significant event in the ongoing history of the University: the inauguration of her seventeenth president, Raleigh Kirby Godsey.

The essays presented herein reflect a variety of backgrounds and traditions, and suggest a broad ecumenical perspective. They record the thoughtful analyses and convictions of a distinguished group of educators who share Mercer's long-standing commitment to the integration of faith and learning. They propose reassessment of the church-related university in a new era, relating some of the concerns, aspirations, challenges, risks, and rewards of Christian higher education as it charts new pathways for the future. We express deep appreciation to the essayists for sharing here their insights and anticipations.

We have been fortunate to have the services of Dr. Ben C. Fisher as editor of this volume. He has long been identified in the academic world as a prominent leader in Baptist higher education, and as a guide and challenger of Southern Baptist educational institutions. The participation of notable educators as essayists indicates that they share our respectful regard and appreciation for him. We express to him our gratitude for his contribution to this venture, and to Mrs. Fisher warm thanks for her helpful editorial assistance.

The idea of this book was conceived by Dr. Watson E. Mills, Director of the Mercer University Press. He also furnished its title, and his skilled hand guided it through the technical processes of production. To him we express abundant appreciation for his tireless labor.

The Committee for the Inauguration
Harold L. McManus, *Chairman*

List of Contributors

James S. Barrett is the Associate General Secretary, Division of Higher Education, Board of Higher Education and Ministry of the United Methodist Church, Nashville, Tennessee. He received his education at Wofford College, Emory University, Columbia Theological Seminary, and the University of Georgia. Dr. Barrett has also served as pastor in South Carolina churches, and as a college administrator at Spartanburg Methodist College.

Grady C. Cothen is President of the Sunday School Board of the Southern Baptist Convention. He has served as president of Oklahoma Baptist University and New Orleans Baptist Theological Seminary. He is a frequent contributor to professional and religious journals and is the author of *God of the Beginnings, Faith and Higher Education* and *Unto All the World: Bold Mission*.

R. Kirby Godsey is President of Mercer University. (See pages 1-3 for additional biographical information).

E. Eugene Hall is President of Oklahoma Baptist University. He has served as associate professor in the speech departments of Louisiana College, Georgetown College, and Western Kentucky University. In addition, he was dean of the College, then vice president for academic affairs at Louisiana College. Dr. Hall was editor of the *Kentucky Journal of Communication Arts*.

Fred E. Harris is President of West Virginia Wesleyan College in Buckhannon, West Virginia. He has served as dean at Baldwin-Wallace College, vice president for academic affairs at the University of Evansville, associate general secretary of the Division of Higher Education of the United Methodist Board of Higher Education and Ministry, faculty member at the University of Kentucky, and secretary-treasurer and member of the board of the National Foundation for Christian Higher Education.

L. D. Johnson is Chaplain and Professor of Religion at Furman University. He has served as pastor of the First Baptist Church of Danville, Virginia, as chairman of the department of religion of the University of Richmond, and as pastor of the First Baptist Church of Greenville, South Carolina. He is the author of four books: *An Introduction to the Bible, Out of the Whirlwind, Israel's Wisdom: Learn and Live*, and *The Morning After Death*.

Abner V. McCall is President of Baylor University. He is a past president of the Association of Southern Baptist Colleges and Schools, the Independent Colleges and Universities of Texas, Inc., the Association of Texas Colleges and Universities, and the Texas Foundation of Voluntarily Supported Colleges and Universities.

John F. Murphy is the Executive Director of the Association of Catholic Colleges and Universities. He served as vice president for university relations at the Catholic University of America and president of Thomas More College in Covington, Kentucky. He was named a Monsignor by Pope John XXIII in 1960.

Dallin H. Oaks is President of Brigham Young University. He is also professor of law in BYU's J. Reuben Clark Law School. He has served as a law clerk to Chief Justice Earl Warren of the United States Supreme Court. He is also the author of over 50 articles published in legal and other periodicals and magazines, and has been on the editorial boards of several professional journals.

Richard W. Solberg is Director of the Department for Higher Education of the Lutheran Church in America. He has served as vice president for academic affairs and professor of history at Thiel College in Greenville, Pennsylvania. He is the author of three books: *God and Caesar in East Germany, As Between Brothers,* and *How Church-Related Are Church Related Colleges?*

Arthur L. Walker, Jr., is Executive Director-Treasurer of the Education Commission of the Southern Baptist Convention. He has served as vice president for student affairs at both the Southern Baptist Theological Seminary and Samford University. He has written widely for denominational publications and was a contributor to the *Encyclopedia of Southern Baptists.*

About the Editor

Ben C. Fisher is a consultant for the Education Commission of the Southern Baptist Convention and an adjunct professor of religion and educational consultant at Campbell University. He has served as executive director-treasurer of the Education Commission and secretary-treasurer of the Commission on the American Baptist Theological Seminary. He has also served as director of the North Carolina Association of Independent Colleges and Universities. He has written numerous articles, has contributed to denominational and religious periodicals, and has served as editor of *Southern Baptist Educator.* In February of 1980 he was given the distinguished service award from the National Association of Independent Colleges and Universities "for his contributions to American higher education."

Table of Contents

Raleigh Kirby Godsey
Seventeenth President of Mercer University

Raleigh Kirby Godsey
A Biographical Sketch

Arthur L. Walker, Jr.

"Unless a person dreams, he becomes a victim of the way things are . . . . Unless our activity is punctuated with the vision of where we are going, we will begin very quickly to go nowhere."

The truth of these words must have been planted in the mind of their author very early, for Kirby Godsey has been a dreamer all his life, refusing to accept things as they are. His dreams, however, have been steeped in the realities of determination and hard work. "No amount of vision or ability will be productive unless we are willing to invest energy and commitment." The truth of these words is borne out by his personal, academic, and professional accomplishments in two score years and three.

Raleigh Kirby Godsey was born April 2, 1936, in Birmingham, Alabama. He was graduated from Samford University (then Howard College) with a B.A. in history in 1957. Three years later, he received a B.D. degree from New Orleans Baptist Theological Seminary, and remained at the seminary for further study while also serving as pastor of the Norwood (Louisiana) Baptist Church.

After receiving the Doctor of Theology degree in 1962, Godsey became assistant professor of philosophy and religion at Judson College in Marion, Alabama. His teaching experience was interspersed with continued formal learning, culminating in the M. A. degree in philosophy from the University of Alabama in 1967.

From Marion, Godsey returned to New Orleans in 1967 and received the Ph.D. in philosophy from Tulane University in 1969. He was then invited to Averett College by Dr. Conwell Anderson under whose presidency he had earlier taught at Judson. Anderson asked him to be dean of Averett and later wrote of his service: "He took to the deanship with enthusiasm and skill. He planned well, sold his ideas effectively, and was outstanding in interpersonal relations." As dean and vice president of

Averett from 1969 to 1977, Godsey was an example of his own administrative philosophy: "The people who make a difference are those who will work harder. Leadership is not a spectator sport."

Never content to be a spectator, his leadership brought recognition. He was listed among the Outstanding Young Men of America in 1965 and again in 1970. He received the Danville Citizenship Award in 1971. From 1972 to 1975 he served as chairman of the board of directors of the Danville School of the Arts. He served also as a member of state committees on health planning and educational needs for the State of Virginia. Public speaking opportunities were innumerable. Civic organizations soon heard of his wit, perception, and good sense. Churches were impressed with preaching that reflected dedication to Christ and theological clarity. Peer groups in educational circles responded to his enthusiasm for education and professional understanding.

It may be admitted that some of his community responsibilities while in Danville resulted from his desire to provide improved educational and cultural opportunities for his own talented young family and the families of colleagues and community friends. His involvement in cultural interests was doubtless inevitable because of the talents and cultural concerns of Joan Stockstill Godsey. At the time of their marriage in 1959 she was a member of the music faculty at New Orleans Baptist Theological Seminary and was then, as now, a highly accomplished musician.

Academic administration gave Godsey many new opportunities. Under his leadership Averett College expanded its curriculum and increased its student body. He served as chairman of a task force on academic affairs for the Council for the Advancement of Small Colleges. He lectured on personnel relations and academic leadership and spoke at numerous local, state, and regional educational and religious conferences. He wrote and taught in philosophy and religion. Among the subjects on which he published articles were the ontology of education, the relevance of philosophy to the social sciences, aspects of Whiteheadian philosophy, and the importance of Christian higher education on the American educational scene.

In 1977 Godsey accepted the invitation to become the Dean of the College of Liberal Arts of Mercer University. This role gave him the opportunity to bring to bear upon one of the older Baptist institutions of higher education his broad range of experiences and talents. At Mercer he has been able to apply his experience as chief consultant for the Comprehensive Institutional Development Project (funded by the United States Office of Education); representative of the Higher Educational Panel of the American Council on Education; chairman of the Conference on Institutional Planning (sponsored by the American Association of Higher Education); consultant for problems relating to the management of Higher Education and Organizational Development; and as a member of the Directing Committee of the National Workshop on Faculty Development (sponsored by the Lilly and Kellogg foundations).

Godsey is one of those people who make a difference. In 1978 he was named Executive Vice President of Mercer University and when President Rufus C. Harris announced his retirement, Godsey was an obvious candidate for consideration as the seventeenth president of the institution. Frenetic activities may bring recognition but active participation with thoughtful commitment brings lasting results. It is obvious that Kirby Godsey has pursued the latter. The many involvements of his life have lasting consequence. This is reflected in the achievements of his charming and talented daughters, Stephanie and Erica, and his studious and achieving sons, Hunter and Raleigh. It is also reflected in the respect of his colleagues. Those with whom he has taught or served in educational endeavors take pride in that relationship.

At the National Conference on Bold Christian Education and Bold Missions sponsored by the Education Commission of the Southern Baptist Convention and the Association of Southern Baptist Colleges and Schools in 1979, Godsey delivered one of the major addresses. In that address he stressed that a Christian university has the obligation to deal honestly with its purpose and its parent Christian body in the task of presenting knowledge and values. The key emphasis of that address is also the key to understanding the new president of Mercer University, and his desire to commit the university to academic integrity and Christian purpose.

Introduction

On a cold, blustery day, December 16, 1977, twenty-two heads of boards of church-related higher education walked the short distance from Number One Dupont Circle to the White House to keep an appointment with the President of the United States. The meeting had been postponed once because of the President's involvement with the national budget. At the beginning of the week, the Israeli-Egyptian crisis had deepened, and Prime Minister Menachem Begin was a guest at the White House. The long awaited conference seemed again in jeopardy, but President Carter refused to cancel our appointment, and met with us for nearly an hour.

The statement he made was brief, but it was the strongest endorsement of church-related higher education ever made by any American government leader, expressing appreciation for the contribution of these institutions and urging that their service to the nation be recognized and their needs be more adequately met.

We cite this as only one evidence of resurgent interest in church-related colleges and universities. There are many other signs of renewed hope.

A recent report in the *Chronicle of Higher Education* indicates that the largest gain in enrollment in the private sector for the 1979-80 term took place in church-related schools. In 1976 Earl J. McGrath, executive director of the Program in Liberal Studies at the University of Arizona, did a careful enrollment study in church-related colleges, and at that time predicted that enrollments were likely to increase in those church-related institutions which remain committed to their Christian purpose and to their sponsoring denomination.

One of the strongest indications of renewed vitality in church-related higher education is to be found in a number of significant studies made recently by church groups themselves. *Church-Related Higher Education,* by Robert Rue Parsonage, is one of the best of these current publications because it summarizes many of the findings in articles and books listed below. Within the past five years all major denominations and many of the smaller religious bodies have made extensive professional surveys of their educational institutions, reaffirming concern and support.[1]

---

[1] See such important studies as *The Quest for a Viable Saga: The Church-Related College in an Age of Pluralism,* a study by Baepler, Narum, Olsen, Stenshoel, and

A high-water mark for Southern Baptist colleges and schools was the National Colloquium held in Williamsburg, Virginia, in 1976. This meeting drew more than 800 delegates representing all facets of Southern Baptist leadership.

Along with other hopeful signs which seem to be promising a brighter day for Christian higher education has come a fresh approach to ecumenism, based primarily upon the recognition that our unity must remain in diversity. At Notre Dame University in June, 1979, and again in Washington, D.C., in February, 1980, a National Congress was held on church-related higher education, supported by twenty-three denominations representing more than a hundred million church members. The positive impact of these meetings is already being felt. As children of God we are finding new ties that bind us together in the lordship of Christ, in the authority of the scriptures, and in our belief in life eternal. We are also finding renewed joy in commitment to missions, evangelism, social concerns, and a Christian world view. Furthermore, we are discovering a new strength and a new sense of purpose as we battle together the ever-growing tide of secularism and the consequent erosion of Christian values.

Therefore, believing that it *is* a new day, and that we need not only to find new pathways but to walk old pathways with fresh insights, a number of nationally known scholars and educators, not only among Baptists but from other denominations as well, have been asked to write the various chapters which comprise this volume. The book reflects many foci of concern, and is a

Vos for the Association of Lutheran College Faculties; Charles R. Bruning's *Relationships Between Church-Related Colleges and Their Constituencies: A Review of the Literature* (Lutheran Church in America); "The Catholic University in the Modern World," statement of the Second International Congress of Delegates of the Catholic Universities of the World; *A College-Related Church: United Methodist Perspectives; Endangered Service: Independent Colleges, Public Policy and the First Amendment* (National Commission on United Methodist Higher Education); Francis C. Gamelin's *Church-Related Identity of Lutheran Colleges* (Lutheran Educational Conference of North America); Earl J. McGrath's *Study of Southern Baptist Colleges and Universities, 1976-77;* Moots and Gaffney's *Church & Campus; Project I: The Jesuit Apostolate of Education in the United States, National Consultation;* and *Reaffirmations, Adopted by the Association of Southern Baptist Colleges and Schools.* See also the important new (1980) four-volume series by the National Congress on Church-Related Colleges and Universities, under the general title *Church and College: A Vital Partnership* (Vol. I, *Affirmation;* Vol. II, *Mission;* Vol. III, *Accountability;* and Vol. IV, *Exchange).*

highly appropriate part of the inaugural celebration for Dr. R. Kirby Godsey, president of Mercer University, whose dynamic concept of church-related higher education is skillfully delineated in the first chapter. Subjects range from the wide topic of Christian unity in diversity to specific suggestions for development of values-centered curriculum and campus ministry; and from such broad challenges as secularism and loss of national purpose to detailed discussions of the mission of a Baptist university, its role as an institution of the church, and its relation to the denomination. Of no less importance are the two chapters dealing with freedom and the preservation of pluralism in American higher education.

There was a time when the role of the American university was relatively simple and widely accepted. Under a general concept of education resting largely upon English and German tradition, curricula were reasonably uniform, and colleges and universities could be fairly sure of what was expected of them— by students, faculty, the supporting constituency, and society in general.

But for more than a decade now, the word used most frequently in connection with higher education has been *crisis*. The crises have been described in many categories, including purpose, finance, curriculum, government control, student revolution, governance, and the emergence of new, competitive types of education sponsored outside of the college and university. The tendency has often been for the university, reeling and buffeted by all this change, to become defensive and simply to try to conform to the new expectations, yielding especially at the points of highest pressure.

What is needed now is for the institution of higher learning, in its critical position of intellectual leadership, to look clear-eyed at the total picture, evaluate what is expected of higher education in the complexity of these times, and decide what its responsibilities actually are and ought to be. Out of this long struggle and these recurring traumas, thoughtful educators should be able to re-focus on institutional purpose and goals.

Nowhere in American higher education is there greater freedom and greater flexibility to seize upon opportunities than in the church-related college. Therefore it is particularly fitting that an institution such as Mercer University should honor its new president by taking the initiative to publish this book of suggestions for new pathways that church-related higher education may travel.

Ben C. Fisher
March, 1980

I. New Pathways

The Mission of Mercer University: A Blueprint for the Future

R. Kirby Godsey

The mission of Mercer University deserves strong and clear articulation. As a private university, we carry both the advantage and the burden of a heavy responsibility for the identification and implementation of our mission. Unlike the public sector, the private university does not derive its purpose from the electorate or the state or any other extrinsic source. We determine our own meaning and purpose and validate our own reason for being.

It is important, then, for us to understand our nature as an institution of higher learning since each college and school of the university seeks to fulfill that mission in ways that bring specific means for the implementation of the university's mission. The worth and the significance of each enterprise of the university must be judged by our common understanding of that mission, the consciousness of which can bring a measure of vitality and self-directed planning that cannot be achieved in any other way. Furthermore, the mission becomes the operating criterion by which programs are judged as to their propriety and worth to this particular academic community. Without that clarity, each college is left to pursue its own work without reference to the destiny of the university. In contrast, a consciousness of the university's mission suggests that the emergence of each school is intimately tied to the emergence of the other schools and colleges.

The existence of institutional mission also provides the only reasonable context for planning since meaningful planning is a contextual undertaking. Good planning takes into account a range of resources, including financial, human, and ideological resources, that surround an institution. But planning remains nothing more than a collection of alternatives unless it is rooted in a clear and commonly agreed upon understanding of what the university is about. Mission must prevail in our planning.

The mission of the university has a strong historical basis, and that history can be very instructive for the statement of mission today. Because of its nature, the mission of an institution must remain stable. It cannot shift with the daily changes of perspectives and personnel. The mission anchors the institution against such shifts.

Statements of mission must be broad to include the entire spectrum of the university's work and at the same time provide the boundaries for the pursuit of the specific endeavors of each college.

As a basis for continuing thought and conversation and as an indication of my own perceptions, I here set forward my own understanding of:

A.   The historical and enduring mission of the university;

B.   The aims of education that guide the learning programs of the university;

C.   The managing objectives by which this administration is seeking to enter its work.

Historical and Enduring Mission of the University

In my own study and reflection upon the history and development of Mercer University, I find that Mercer does indeed have a historical identity that can be stated very succinctly. Mercer University is a church-related institution of higher learning, providing both liberal and professional education that seeks to achieve excellence and discipline in the fields of liberal learning and professional knowledge joined with an explicit concern for presenting the Christian understanding of the world and a compassionate community that undergirds the students' pursuit of knowledge, human meaning, and moral values.

This statement suggests to me that Mercer University is first of all an institution of learning. That primary issue must remain pervasive, because learning and inquiry are the focus of our work. The conferring of degrees becomes a public declaration of the institution's fulfillment of this inviolable aspect of its mission. All research, all public service, all personnel decisions of the university are finally justified by whether they contribute to the achievement of learning. The preparation for work, the addressing of social or community problems, the development of curricula must serve the end of learning and inquiry. Learning is both an intrinsic and instrumental good. That is to say, learning can be done for the sake of learning itself, and learning is also undertaken for the sake of preparation to address other problems and to perform other responsibilities. In either case, learning remains crucial to the identity of the university.

The review of our historical mission also teaches us that the meaning of Mercer carries specific and deliberate reference to the Christian faith. The lives of Baptist colleges and universities are deeply intertwined with the birth and unfolding of a missionary consciousness. These colleges were not conceived in abstraction. They did not spring fullborn from the churches and conventions that birthed them. They were raised as instruments of change. They were born as ways by which the outreach of the church and the fledgling concerns for missions could become more effective. Baptist education needs to examine its roots, not to create a past but to recover a past. We had better examine our moorings. If we want to know where we are going, let us not be afraid to look at the tracks we have made.

Be sure of this fact—the story of Baptists is the story of the interactive development of three certain and clear areas: religious liberty, missions, and education. Mercer University is founded solidly upon the faith of Christians who call themselves Baptists, and the university has undertaken its mission as an expression of Christian responsibility.

Consequently, Mercer exists as an institution of higher education in which teaching and learning are brought together with the growth and the development of the human spirit as a principal element of the educational process. Therefore, at the center of its mission lies the commitment to pursue learning and inquiry in a setting where Christian values and the moral life are serious issues for study and learning. There is no learning that does not involve what a person believes. The university is **not** Christian in the sense that it aims to impose the Christian faith upon any student or any member of the university community. We must keep alive the ability of those who hear us to turn another way without ourselves turning away and taking away our care and commitment to help. Mercer *is* a Christian university in the sense that it springs from Christian responsibility that comes to life in being concerned, not only for matters of abstract inquiry, but for matters of personal meaning and integrity. It is a place where thought and belief remain bound together with an awesome consciousness that all history and nature is pervaded with the presence of Holiness.

There are lessons of the spirit: We are learning to fly through the air faster than the breaking of day; and that's good, but it is not enough. We are learning to link up thinking machines and human minds; and that's good, but it is not enough. We are learning to communicate around the world with incredible speed and precision; and that's good, but it is not enough unless we have something to say. The lesson of the spirit is this: Ours is not an issue of intelligence; it is an issue of wisdom. The question is **not** whether we know enough but whether we are good enough to keep our world together.

The work of the university remains only one of the many deeply formative experiences in any student's life. The university stands alongside other forces within the social order in the development of the human mind and the human character. The university's work is aided by other social institutions, such as the media, the peer group, the church, and the family who contribute to an overall life perspective. We pursue our own mission aware that our work affects and is affected by a great many other forces. We should, therefore, not claim too much for ourselves nor diminish our own burden. In my judgment, the mission of Mercer University is about learning and the unfolding of the human spirit, and we operate within the conviction that the pursuit of learning and the consideration of faith can strengthen the human capacity for judgment in addressing the problems that complicate our world.

The Aims of Education

The aims of education can be usefully distinguished from the mission of the university. The mission sets the identity of the institution. It expresses the ideological counterpart to the legal charter, the *raison d'être* of the university. On the other hand, the aims of education begin the process of defining in a more particular way how the mission actually operates within the program of the university. The aims of education set forward the goals of the educational program, even though these goals are also necessarily general since they provide the criteria by which the educational process may be assessed and judged as to its quality. The following paragraphs suggest some of the aims that should govern the educational processes of Mercer University. These are not stated with either finality or exclusiveness but rather as a reflection of my own thoughts about some of the guiding forces of education here. Most of these aims are addressed not only at Mercer but at other educational, as well as social, institutions. Nevertheless, they do serve as very basic goals that we are seeking to achieve.

1. *To develop the ability to think more clearly and precisely.*

Human thought represents a fundamental aspect of the human experience. We are thinking, reasoning creatures. One of the aims of learning is to sharpen the students' ability to reason cogently. Most of the problems we face are subject to rational analysis. The ability to make judgments based upon reason and thought will constitute an elementary characteristic of the educated person.

2. *To heighten the ability to use language more effectively.*

As one of the aims of education, language should be understood very broadly. We need not overlook the fact that people need to use the written and verbal word with precision and attention to meaning. There are, of course, many other "languages" or forms of symbolic communication. Education should strengthen the individual's power of communication. This process must begin long before college, but colleges and universities bear responsibility for continued growth and development.

3. *To cultivate the ability to solve problems more effectively.*

One of the aims of education that should be achieved in each of the colleges and schools is enabling a person to harness what he knows toward the solution of problems. The university fails when its students do not become better problem solvers through their years of formal education.

4. *To enhance the students' ability to analyze data, to compare, and to extrapolate.*

Each person continually faces a host of undifferentiated data in his experience. We perceive more than we understand. A part of the process of education is to strengthen a person's ability to bring order and definition to the range of information which experience provides and to be able to separate the important from the trivial components of that data.

5. *To increase the capacity for self-transcendence.*

The educated person recognizes his limitations and seeks to maintain some measure of distance from his own ideas and beliefs. Otherwise, his own actions and opinions seem to take on a quality of infallibility that is not conducive to the continuation of learning or the development of wisdom.

6. *To enhance the ability to listen.*

In my view one of the better signs of an educated person is the ability to listen. Listening can take many forms -- reading, watching, or hearing. Listening requires a heightened awareness that knowledge is limited and incomplete; it requires also a willingness to change, acknowledging the value and importance of another person and his ideas. It often requires more confidence to listen than to speak.

7. *To enable a person to learn how to learn.*

One of the more important aims of education is to improve the students' ability to gain knowledge with initiative and independence. Learning to learn suggests that there are many ways to know. Those ways include conceptual, creative reflection; empirical learning based upon observation and experimentation; analytic reasoning, whether historical, logical or physical analysis; esthetic sensitivity, which may include intuitive and non-rational knowledge or awareness; and relational concepts which may include knowledge that is principally a result of relationships themselves. Whatever the means of knowing, education should enable a person to become a more effective learner.

8. *To enlarge the capacity for informed judgments and discriminating moral choices.*

A very important aim for education with the educational setting of this university pertains to the issues of moral judgment. The university addresses as a primary goal the issues of moral value and personal decision-making as well as matters of meaning and integrity within the social order.

9. *To understand the impact of religious commitments upon learning and work.*

As a principal part of its undertaking this university addresses the relationship of faith and reason, of believing and knowing. The development of belief and ultimate religious perspectives remains very much a part of making decisions about one's life and work. Education is in the business of growing people, of addressing what is ultimately important and real to them. This university aims toward providing a context in which a student may face questions of religious meaning. The aim of education cannot be to impose these commitments on any student, but rather to provide a learning community where the interaction between faith and intellect may be explored.

10. *To contribute to the preservation, dissemination and advancement of knowledge.*

One of the aims of education is to preserve and to advance the world of inquiry. Education is an important means for advancing human knowledge, for disseminating what is known, and for pressing back the horizons of the unknown. The educational community has been a primary arena for research and development of knowledge in every area of human exploration.

We recognize that education is a social undertaking. This university was founded and is sustained by a community of people who understand that the destiny of the world order resides in the ideas and the will of people. In my judgment, we cannot risk the future of the world to the under-developed human mind or spirit whether in our faith, in our governance, or in our work. Mercer University pursues its educational programs with the confidence that the person educated of mind and spirit can make the most effective contribution toward solving problems that face humankind and toward the ultimate realization of the will of God in history.

Managing Objectives of the University

The primary mission of the university and the aims of education are expressed in certain objectives that we wish to be present in the operation of the colleges and schools as well as the university itself.

The operating objective of Mercer University is to be a comprehensive university of approximately 5,000 students characterized by:

> Institutional integrity that expresses the university's primary commitment to Christian values and relationship to the Baptists of Georgia;
>
> Academic achievement which earns a reputation for educational quality and leadership;
>
> A rational administrative system in which decision-making and policy formation is accessible and responsive to the primary constituencies related to the university; and
>
> Organizational effectiveness which achieves maximum benefits from the integration and investment of its human and material resources.

II. New Pathways

Christian Unity and Diversity

John F. Murphy

T he general title of this series of essays suggests an explorer's tentative map rather than a handsome, five-color layout that documents a well-financed and photographed National Geographic expedition. And I have no disagreement with that. There is indeed something fresh and new and even tentative about the way we are looking at Christian higher education these days. I believe that in itself is Christian, searching out new ground with an inquiring mind and eye. The gospel values we have had for a long time, but the circumstances of now are new, and new pathways need to be cut and explored.

The tumultuous experiences which higher education has endured almost continually since the mid-sixties have left a deep imprint on institutions related to the Christian churches. Even without an academic seismograph we know some "future shocks" are on the way, too, particularly in enrollments and operational costs. There will probably be other convulsive movements which will take us by surprise, as our skill at seeing around corners has doubtless not improved all that much since we were surprised by the sixties and the seventies, a point well documented by

Martin Marty in his valued contribution to *Church-Related Higher Education*.[1]

Nonetheless, the other contributors to this volume, distinguished educators all, do not hesitate to face up to the tough problems that are on the way, and to whistle up a bit of courage about those that are surely there but as yet unidentified! Whether buoyed by the sturdy virtue of Christian hope, or merely responding as a battered, rubber-legged fighter to one more ring of the bell, my colleagues (many are dear friends) will serve the readers well in pointing and warning and evaluating.

Mine is a different task, one that has inspired saints and martyrs, and that has occasionally been the cause of both—i.e., their sanctity and their martyrdom! I am to write about ecumenism in Christian higher education or, rather, how Christians as colorfully different as Joseph's coat might find a unity we have not previously enjoyed amid a well-known diversity which we treasure and want to celebrate.

I am encouraged in this task first by the ultimately infallible prayer of Jesus that we might all be one as He is one in the Father (John 17:21). Despite the heartbreaks, scandals, and failures of the past, there is no question that we can discern in our times a new movement of Christians toward one another. May God be praised for that! It is obviously not the direct responsibility of our institutions, precisely as colleges, to be charged with the larger ecumenical task of the churches, or even the smaller task of the individual Christian. But we in the Christian colleges can take advantage of the new environment of openness and trust which has been created; and the experiences and cooperation we share can in turn provide assistance to the work of our parent bodies, and inspiration to our individual members.

I am further encouraged by the remarkable events in which many of us have recently participated; namely, those of the National Congress on Church-Related Colleges and Universities, sponsored by twenty-three Christian denominations and their institutions.[2] In the work of this

---

[1] Robert Rue Parsonage, ed., *Church-Related Higher Education* (Valley Forge: Judson, 1978), pp. 303-304.

[2] An eighteen-month program of Study Commissions and two general assemblies, one at the University of Notre Dame in June, 1979, and a concluding session in Washington in February, 1980.

Congress we found a common cause which we had not previously fully sensed. We did in fact celebrate the diversity, as we found opportunity to observe how Christian inspiration, embodied in different traditions, has brought forth a great cornucopia of Christian educational benefits. In studying and working and praying with one another we did indeed find and experience a new Christian unity.

Strengthened by faith in the prayer of Jesus and by movements of the Spirit already seen and marveled at in our own time, I suggest that all who have responsibility for Christian colleges, and who love the Lord and seek the unity He wills, might begin to consider some guideposts as we step down these new paths of the future—a future which is already upon us.

The Recognition of Common Cause in Matters of Public Policy

In an energy-conscious period we could call this first guidepost a "share-the-ride" program. We have some mutual concerns among our denominational colleges; we are traveling the same road. Why go alone? We can gain strength from united efforts. We can spread our limited resources further. I prefer to term this Christian pragmatism. Self-interest opens our eyes to the help we can exchange with our neighbor. It is not the ultimate in ecumenism; but it is not a bad place to begin.

The Study Action Committee which guided the important study that was published under the name *Church-Related Higher Education*, adding some final words about the project, concluded in the last sentence of the book, "Immediate attention needs to be given to the whole matter of formulation and support of an ecumenical basis of public policy congenial to church-related higher education and its purposes."[3]

Some important progress has already been made. While the National Association of Independent Colleges and Universities (taken from the side of the Association of American Colleges in 1976) organizes its members as independent and includes many with no church relationship, many of the interests of the church-related sector are met quite effectively. NAICU staff and board, as well as NAICU members, have been quite open to promoting any issues of special concern to the members with church ties.

---

[3]Parsonage, p. 341.

Much collaboration is still needed in areas usually related to First Amendment questions. Skilled defenders of the rights of church-related institutions and of those who attend and teach in them are now being heard where formerly only a secularist viewpoint predominated. The work of Philip Moots and Edward McGlynn Gaffney of the Center for Constitutional Studies at the University of Notre Dame should be mentioned. Mr. Gaffney is probing the current "rationalistic mold of education which the Court appears to have blessed as the only educational endeavor worthy of public support."[4] President Dallin Oaks of Brigham Young University is contending that individual rights to free exercises of religion may be endangered unless institutional rights are recognized.[5]

Dr. Landrum Bolling, speaking at the closing assembly of the National Congress on Church-Related Colleges and Universities this last February, strongly supported the earlier assertions of Peter Berger and Richard Neuhaus regarding the value of "mediating institutions"[6] and called for a more balanced view of the First Amendment than is reflected in current court decisions or in administrative law and regulations.

Notre Dame's Center for Constitutional Studies has met with admirable interdenominational support, and can perhaps serve as a model of collaboration which could be duplicated in other areas on other university campuses.

An On-Going Probe by the Institutions of Their Own Mission

It may appear curious, but the first gift to be brought to an ecumenical endeavor is a clear understanding of one's own tradition. As we Christians humbly continue the pilgrimage together towards a new unity, we bring along the riches of our own history. Christians in higher education need a thorough inventory of their own luggage. What inspired Lutherans or

---

[4]"The Constitution and the Campus: the Case for Institutional Integrity and the Need for Critical Self-Evaluation," in *Church and College: A Vital Partnership;* Vol. 3: *Accountability—Keeping Faith With One Another* (Sherman, Texas: The National Congress on Church-Related Colleges and Universities 1980), p. 57.

[5]W. Cole Durham, Jr., "Constitutional Protections for Independent Higher Education: Limited Powers and Institutional Rights," in *ibid.,* Chap. five.

[6]Cf. *To Empower People: The Role of Mediating Structures in Public Policy* (New York: American Enterprise Institute, 1977).

Methodists in higher education efforts? Although there has been much commendable reflection on institutional mission in recent years, the process is never completed. There remains a continuing obligation to evaluate each unique religious viewpoint alongside the circumstances of our times.

Given the overwhelming secularization of present-day higher education, there is always a risk that we may forget that we must be different. In Merrimon Cuninggim's apt phrase, "We are not talking about a specific function of the church; we are talking, instead, about a specific kind of college."[7] Later, in that same essay, he lists essentials for any institution which is church-related. But each denomination, even each institution, must apply the criteria in a way that is proper to its own vision of mission. One excellent outcome of our recent Congress is the inventory of church-relatedness which contains enough to keep administrators and faculty, trustees and church leaders in healthy debate for a long time, until new affirmations arise and the course for the future is reset.

I believe that all of us will find there is need for reform and renewal if we are to be faithful both to the roots of the past and to the present moment. We should not fear that searching self-analysis. Nor should we fear, once judgment has been passed, to take the brave steps to implement renewal. *We each need to risk being fully Christian, or we risk being nothing.* The lukewarm were not among the Lord's favorites.

The Fathers of the Second Vatican Council, in speaking of the *ecclesia semper reformanda* in their decree on ecumenism, used some encouraging words which have equal applicability to us in church-related colleges.

> Christ summons the Church, as she goes her pilgrim way, to the continual reformation of which she always has need, insofar as she is an institution of men here on earth. Therefore, if the influence of events or of the times has led to deficiencies of conduct. . . , these should appropriately be rectified at the proper moment.[8]

---

[7]Parsonage, p. 17.

[8]*The Documents of Vatican II* (New York: American Press, 1966), p. 350.

Listening and Learning

This guidepost directs us as Christians to listen respectfully to one another, absorbing those aspects of the Christian tradition which are not our own. A delicate prodding of our biblical memory recalls how the Good Samaritan bettered the Pharisee and the Levite as the hero of Jesus' parable. And how Peter went calling on Cornelius after he received in his vision a rather pointed lesson on discrimination (Acts 10).

We have already made some progress in moving from our self-imposed ghettos so that we can see our brothers and sisters as they really are, not as we may have imagined them to be. The prophetic young Christians at Taize speak to us, "We have also seen clearly that, when Christians shut themselves up in rivalries or competition, little by little the common creation is paralyzed."[9] Since, as William Kinnison observes, "Myths function as realities in the behavior and motivation of people,"[10] we all bear a responsibility to de-mythologize our impressions of one another's tradition in higher education. We all must be prepared to acknowledge that there is in fact a plurality of authentic ways in which Christian higher education can be proposed. Just so, no one denomination can claim to have cornered the complete meaning of Christian higher education.

> Let it also be said that Christian church-related college leadership well knows that, however legitimate the present accents may be, they do not express the plenitude of the Christian ethos and outlook. Sooner or later thoughtful people try to recover elements of tradition that are overlooked during a particular societal stress.[11]

We may be beyond much of the hostility and chauvinism which has scarred past relations, but an ever-pressing ecumenical mission calls us to deliberate moves to eliminate every vestige of ignorance that is an obstacle to a joint journey on new paths.

Once having decided to sponsor the National Congress, we were all caught up in its activities and programs. Now that it is completed, with success beyond our expectations, we must be sure that the informal

---

[9] *Letter from Taize,* Feb., 1980.

[10] Parsonage, p. 90.

[11] *Ibid., p. 308.*

structure of relationships among denominational executives in higher education can be effective as a channel of communications among us. For example, just as the Christian churches have in recent years sent official "observers" to one another's major denominational meetings, we who are in higher education may need to do something similar. There is simply no substitute for continuing opportunities to learn about and from one another. It takes considerable time to cut through our language differences to get at the substance of educational philosophy and mission. It will take even longer to absorb the true meaning of others' history.

The Sharing of Projects Related to Christian Mission:
Christians Working Together

The first result of knowing each other better is that we discover that many mission-inspired activities on the campuses of other denominations are similar to those on our own. Opportunities for cooperation emerge. Or, where different initiatives have been undertaken, the observer can borrow and make them his own. In the first category, the work of biblical scholars is an ideal example. Front-line scholars have been collaborating for some years now, with beneficial results for all. These men and women, who have the charge of helping the churches acquire an ever more penetrating understanding of God's word, are in regular scholarly contact. The exchange of biblical researchers and teachers should be continued. My own denomination has found value in having theologians from other communions on our campuses, both to teach the theology of that church, and also to share in teaching that common Christian tradition from which all Christian theology is nourished.

Other areas of opportunity come to mind. Although our Association of Catholic Colleges and Universities has had moderate success in promoting programs of justice education on Catholic campuses, new insights could be discovered by cooperating with others who feel with us that education for justice is an essential component of Christian higher education. We believe that a small network of relationships among neighboring institutions of all denominations could result in a sharing of resources and programs. If we are trying to prepare our students to be men and women of Christian vision who can serve the world they will enter, can we neglect to help form them for lives of justice? "The breath of God is blowing through today's world to such an extent that many are beginning to awaken from passivity in order to take part in a common creation."[12]

I must confess to a desire for a collaboration that reaches across our entire education programs. I have a deep conviction that the crisis of Christian higher education is at the classroom level and in the curriculum, particularly at the undergraduate level. I think there is a pervasive academic secularism which simply threatens to destroy the meaning of Christian higher learning. In the name of academic purity and integrity we have seen the disciplines stripped of the value questions which are proper to them. This point of view has been promoted by the prestigious graduate schools from which we have drawn faculty. It has invaded the church-related campus through these faculty persons, who are either ignorant or neutral about Christian higher education. If the president of the Association of American Colleges can write in obvious alarm: "The common purpose for which we have banded together makes it imperative that we take the initiative in improving the coherence and quality of the educational programs that American colleges and universities offer students,"[13] then, I submit, there is a more compelling reason why Christian educators should group to restore what has often been lost or ignored.

Some contend that religious illiteracy in our country is increasing rapidly. Calling again on Martin Marty's perceptive essay, we read that church-related higher education has been threatened by the religious "experiential" period through which we have been passing, which is long on personal feelings but short on theology and religious knowledge.[14] It cannot be denied that the perceptions of purpose vary among Lutherans and United Methodists and Southern Baptists and Presbyterians and Catholics *et al.*, but we all claim concern about "value-centered education" in a Christian context. We all need all the help we can get from all sources. If only small numbers of faculty members on our campuses sense the urgency of this task, they must be supported in their work lest this generation of Christian colleges and universities, under the real pressures to compromise their purpose, might be compromised out of existence as church-related schools.

---

[12]*Letter from Taize.*

[13]Address of the President, 66th Annual Meeting, January 10-12, 1980.

[14]Parsonage, p. 305.

Emphasis on Building Communities of Faith:
Christians Praying Together

Pope John Paul II has reached out to young people in a challenging and loving way, and they have responded to him with love. One of the marks of a genuinely Catholic university, he has said, is that it is a place which encourages and supports communities of faith among faculty and students. There seems to be some evidence that the youth of our time may be turning away from the "me-first," consumer-oriented society in which the pleasure principle seems paramount, in order to seek solid spiritual values. They are not untouched by the excesses that have enveloped young people since the early sixties, and many of them do not translate a new concern for spiritual values into traditional forms of religious belief and practice. Nonetheless, they are open to God and struggling to find Him, calling to mind St. Augustine's dictum, "You have made us for yourself alone, O God, and our hearts are restless until they rest in you."

I introduce this guidepost on "New Pathways Through Christian Unity and Diversity," however, to make a slightly different point. Whereas, in the past, the faculty and student population in our colleges may have belonged almost exclusively to the sponsoring denomination (I know this was *not* the case among some), the present-day college is likely to have students and faculty from many of the Christian communions. It is their welfare of which I speak. If a person attaches himself or herself to an academic community sponsored by a church, he should expect that it will reflect that denominational view of Christianity and the Christian college. Beyond that, though, should we not try to assume some responsibility to support that person's own traditional Christian attachments? Sometimes this can be done by adding to our campus ministry team persons from the other churches. At other times it can mean inviting clergy from local congregations to attend to the spiritual needs of their own communicants. Always, we should try to communicate to those who join us as students or faculty that we respect and honor their religious beliefs and are anxious to help support them.

Of most importance is that the environment of the campus, the way policies are formed and administered, the respect and concern shown for individuals, the un-self-conscious manner in which faith is expressed and lived—all communicate that people are serious about being Christian. It is quite appropriate that Southern Baptists, gathered in Galveston last June, committed themselves "as Christian educators to confessing openly our personal Christian belief and values which will allow our students to identify with this belief and these values."[15] Whatever the manner in which various traditions manifest their faith in God and their attachment to the gospel and person of Jesus, the ethos of the campus should invite and support a faith response from all members of the community. Administrators can no longer exercise the direct authority over the personal lives of students which once was common on campus. The day of *in loco parentis* codes is past. Happily, this thrusts a new and more authentic Christian responsibility upon all of us; namely, to draw others to the way of Christ by personal example. Our spiritual inertia rebels against that; it was easier for us to tell others how to be Christian than to show them!

A Welcome Sign to the Holy Spirit for Any New Movement to Christian Unity: Christians Hoping Together

We cannot know our scriptures and the history of Christians without acknowledging that weakness and infidelity have separated sons and daughters of the same Father, brothers and sisters of the same Savior. As each new generation comes into contact with Christians who do not pray and work and live as one, those young people are scandalized by our divisions. Their innocence and directness challenge us to heal the differences of ecclesial positions hardened by centuries of apartness. Since most of our campuses are truly ecumenical in their populations, is there not a unique opportunity for us to invite Christians of all persuasions to pray together for that unity which will only come in God's time, but which is so frequently thwarted by the hardness of our own hearts? The Decree on Ecumenism of the Second Vatican Council said,

> There can be no ecumenism worthy of the name without a change of heart. For it is from newness of attitudes (Cf.Eph.

---

[15]*Southern Baptist Educator*, XLIII (No. 6, 1979), 11.

4:23), from self-denial and unstinted love, that yearnings for unity take their rise and grow toward maturity. We should therefore pray to the Divine Spirit for the grace to be genuinely self-denying, humble, gentle in the service of others, and to have an attitude of brotherly generosity toward them.[16]

A most important guidepost to lead us toward unity with respect for a diversity that need not be divisive is that all of our campuses be places where people are encouraged to pray together—especially for unity—waiting for the Spirit of God to move in us and in our church bodies.

Offering and Receiving Friendship: Christians Loving One Another

My final guidepost expresses a very simple and human truth. Loving friends create unity. Loving friends can tolerate diversity. Friendship provides support to struggle along difficult pathways.

The Acts of the Apostles can be considered an account of how the power of God created a unity among the disciples so that the will of Christ for His followers could be achieved. But I wonder whether God did not capitalize upon the dear human friendships of these men and women who had come to know and love and trust one another?

The hundreds of church-related colleges and universities in the United States can move from strength to strength in a renewal of Christian higher education if we who live in them form friendships with each other and provide support for common goals. As our friends at Taize state,

At present, every Christian community is faced with an alternative: either to dare and stimulate a common creation, or to become trapped in oppositions that bring everything to a standstill. So that we may be no longer strangers but friends, so that we may go from mutual ignorance to collaboration, are we going to struggle with a reconciled heart, a heart unified by Christ? He challenges each and every one of us: "Before you approach the altar, first go and be reconciled with your brother."[17]

---

[16] *Documents of Vatican II*, p. 351.

[17] *Letter from Taize*.

We honor an old university and a new president with the essays in this commemorative book. No more, yet no less, responsible than six hundred other institutions and their presidents, this university and its new leader are called by the prayer of Christ and the authentic Christian spirit of many people to step bravely down the new pathways that lie open toward a future unity in a pluralism that does not divide but adds a multi-faceted luster to Christian higher education.

III. New Pathways

Confronting the Growing Challenge of Secularism

Richard W. Solberg

Ith the advent of each new decade, the prophets and the planners of our time emerge with assessments, questions, and predictions geared to a ten-year cycle. As if some magical threshold were being crossed, institutions, governments, and various groups in our society are apprised of looming opportunities or impending dangers, somehow identified with a prescribed time block. Yet in retrospect, it should be apparent that most world-shaking events have not been predicted, and that the great changes in human society are best discerned in the perspective of centuries rather than decades.

It is therefore important, especially for persons and institutions engaged in higher education, that in assessing the role of the church-related college or university in this generation and the future, we recognize ourselves as products as well as critics of western culture, and as heirs of ideas, values, and movements which span many centuries. One of these powerful cultural trends which not only affects us profoundly today as persons and as institutions but at times actually threatens to engulf us is secularism. This is the view which asserts that this-worldly concepts provide a sufficient framework for living and that religion and religious considerations may be ignored.

Widening Influence of Secularism

Ever since the renaissance it has been one of the ironies of history that many of those who have sought to resist the advance of secularism have sought to do so by reaffirming the equally distorted world view of the medieval church, with its two-story universe and its definition of the world as evil. Thus with each successive advance in knowledge and understanding of the natural order, the gap has widened between the heralds of the new age and the defenders of the old.

Yet as the centuries have passed, the contributions of the renaissance, the reformation, the scientific revolution, the enlightenment, the industrial revolution, and the age of technology have become intrinsic parts of western culture shared by both heralds and critics. Occasional efforts have been made to synthesize the emerging modern world view with the Christian faith, but more often the old dichotomy of God vs. the world has dominated. And as man's knowledge and self-assurance have increased, God has become less necessary, and the authority of man's knowledge and power has become preeminent. Secularism has seemed to triumph, while its critics continue to sound plaintive protests from the sidelines, all the while enjoying and affirming its benefits.

New Ways of Bearing Witness

A force as pervasive and powerful as secularism in our culture cannot any longer be described simply as a "challenge." In the late 20th century it has become the dominant feature of our culture. The "New Pathways" we seek, therefore, will be described more appropriately as new ways of bearing witness in the midst of a secularist society to those ultimate truths which affirm God's lordship over all creation and thereby provide dimension and meaning for life which transcend the narrow boundaries of secularism.

The biblical injunction to be *in* the world but not *of* the world, directed to Christian persons, could also be addressed to institutions such as church-related colleges and universities. Educational institutions, more than almost any others, are by definition involved in the world, its exploration, its interpretation, and the preparation of those who are to serve as its stewards. But the crucial question for these institutions and their related churches, as well as for individuals, is the stance they take toward the world in which they live.

Stiff Resistance One Option

Martin Marty calls attention to the several options described by H. Richard Niebuhr in his treatment of Christ and culture.[1] It is possible, he observes, for a person or a college, especially a church-related one, to take the position that Christ and the culture are incompatible. Such an ascetic attitude has been historically expressed in the practice of monasticism, which proclaimed withdrawal from the world as the best way to please God and to achieve holiness. It is no accident that this system flourished in the medieval culture which identified the world with sin and evil, and its rejection with goodness and piety. Marty acknowledges, almost unbelievingly, that there are people today who operate Christian liberal arts colleges with the "Christ against culture" approach. In such institutions one might expect to find religious tests to assure the purity of faculty members, prescribed curricula restricting the teaching of evolution, Marxism, or abnormal psychology, the exclusion of all but an approved list of campus speakers, and rigid rules governing the conduct of both faculty and students. In their effort to screen out secularism and worldliness, such institutions have adopted the narrowest kind of sectarianism.

Transforming Society a Dream

At the opposite end of the spectrum are those persons or institutions which have rejected asceticism and identified themselves with the world around them, believing that it is their mission and that of the gospel to transform society and to establish the kingdom of God here on earth. In an earlier and more optimistic part of the 20th century this view found expression on college campuses through the Student Volunteer Movement and in the pulpit and the marketplace through the social gospel movement. There was something attractive and exciting about this crusading spirit, with its passion for a better society, governed by the laws of God, with poverty outlawed, slums eliminated, and wars abolished.

---

[1]Martin E. Marty, "Future Church-Culture Relations and Their Impact on Church-Related Higher Education—The Student Nexus," in Robert Rue Parsonage, ed., *Church-Related Higher Education* (Valley Forge: Judson, 1978), p. 310.

But the dream of a "Christian century" faded quickly before the grim realities of economic depression, war, genocide, and threats of atomic annihilation. These became instead the hallmarks of the 20th century and the documentation of triumphant secularism.

It is doubtful if any church-related colleges in our day espouse such sweeping millennial expectations. However, it is still true that the advocacy of social change and the reform of society as a proper function of the gospel receive strong support among theologians and others in both colleges and seminaries.

In view of the dominance of secularism in modern American society, the two possible stances toward the secular world thus far described offer very little promise for a significant impact of the church upon society. The ascetic, quietistic approach accepts neither responsibility nor challenge, and finally settles for social irrelevance. The activist approach offers good will and an honest commitment to the betterment of the world, but it is founded on a theology which courts disillusionment by under-estimating the plight of mankind and society and ignoring the real source of its ills.

God Is Lord of All Creation

It remains for the church to assert, even in the face of a dominant secularism, that God is the Lord of all creation, and that his creation is good. Moreover, he has placed it under the stewardship of the whole human family, who bear a divinely ordained responsibility for its care whether they are Christian or not.

It is important that the church and its members be able to articulate this stance in the midst of a secular society, and to act with conviction and compassion as responsible stewards of the world's resources.

According to Luther's interpretation of St. Paul, God has established his rule in two realms, the kingdom of God and the kingdom of this world. In his loving concern for the redemption of mankind, he has revealed himself through Jesus Christ and thereby opened the way for all who believe in him to become children of God and members of his heavenly kingdom. This is the message of the gospel.

But in ways which are not always understood, God also preserves and governs the kingdom of this world. This he does, at least in part, through agencies such as civil government, the family, and other social institutions which provide for the orderly conduct of human relations and prevent societal chaos. There is no intent on God's part to redeem the world through such social structures, limited as they are by sin and subject to human mismanagement.

Christians Serve within Society

Because God is the ruler of both kingdoms, Christian men and women are citizens of both kingdoms. They are not to be separated from the world in some antiseptic fashion, but, together with all people, they are expected to share a civil responsibility for the well-being of society. Motivated by gratitude for the gift of life they have received, they devote themselves as servants of God and man to improve the human condition and to establish justice for all. This is no gospel-centered redemption of society. For Christian people it is rather a ministry of love and service. In performing this service, they ally themselves with all who are moved by reason and conscience to respond, whether Christians or not, as they seek to advance the cause of justice. Such cooperation is pleasing to God, who is concerned for the well-being of his world, as well as for the salvation of his children.

It is in this context that the church may discover its most fruitful new pathways for contending against the pervasive cultural secularism of our day. While its primary and essential task is to proclaim God's special revelation through Jesus Christ for the salvation of all people, the church also has access to tremendous human resources and powerful instruments which can be directed toward the achievement of human justice and well-being.

Church-Related Colleges a Resource

Among the best of these resources are the church-related colleges, more than 700 of which are spread across this country. Only recently 23 denominations, representing over 100 million members, sent representatives to a National Congress on Church-Related Colleges and Universities in Washington, D.C., to affirm the importance of these institutions to the church, and the essential character of their past contributions to the life of our country and to its future leadership.

If the full potential of this contribution is to be realized, it is essential that both colleges and churches understand the crucial nature of the role which can be played by a church-related college. On this matter, as indicated earlier in this chapter, views differ widely.

Church Concept of College as Partner

In its effort to define the role of colleges within its understanding of the nature of the church and its ministry, and of God's concern for his creation, the Lutheran Church in America has chosen to describe its colleges as institutional partners with the church. Although entrusted with different tasks, both church and college are accountable to God for the fidelity of their efforts.

According to an official statement adopted by the church in 1976, the primary function of the college is education, a God-ordained but non-redemptive activity, grounded in the first article of the creed, concerning creation.

> The capacity to learn—to search into the secrets of nature and use its resources, to search into the mystery of the human and perceive our misery and our grandeur, to search into the riddle of history and be stalkers of meaning—is possible because of God's goodness. The fact that sinners are not justified by knowledge or cultural refinement should not obscure the further fact that education is the gift of a loving Creator. Through it he would enhance and enrich people's lives. Through it he would inform, motivate, and equip them to make human society what he intends it to be. Sound scholarship, careful research, and effective teaching do him honor and serve his cause. This perception of education, grounded in the theology of the Lutheran church, establishes the freedom and significance of educational institutions. It affirms the college as a college, devoted to its primary task, blending together the differeing talents and convictions of many persons.

[2]"A Statement of the Lutheran Church in America: The Basis for Partnership Between Church and College" (New York: Lutheran Church in America, 1976).

Emphasis on Values a Prime Need

If any significant impact is to be made by church-related higher education within a society dominated by secularism, it will not be enough for churches to define such expectations for the colleges. There must also be a declaration of goals and purposes on the part of the colleges which affirm a similar intent. It is not enough for a college to claim "independence," whether from state or church. It must also proclaim and demonstrate independence from the heavy hand of secularism, which has placed its mark on most of American higher education, including much of the church-related sector. A significant part of the impact of the German university system in America has been the emphasis on objectivity as an ideal in scholarship and in teaching. Hand in hand with this has gone the ideal of "value-free" teaching and learning, as if facts themselves could be established without reference to any scale of importance or system of meaning.

Through the graduate schools of American universities, from which most colleges, including church-related institutions, have drawn their faculty members, this mythical concept of "value-free" education has come to permeate higher learning in this country. Even such humanistic educational leaders in the private sector as Harvard's President Derek Bok, writing in *Daedalus* (Fall, 1974) on the purposes of undergraduate education, seemed reluctant to affirm the validity of values education in colleges.

Among the five major purposes of higher education cited by the Carnegie Commission report of 1973 was the "critical evaluation of society for the sake of society's self-renewal."[3] In its assessment of performance by American colleges and universities in fulfilling these five purposes, the commission gave marks of "adequate," "improving," or "superior" to all but one, namely, the one just cited. Performance on this purpose was described as "quite uneven in the past and uncertain for the future." The absence, or at least the uncertainty of standards of judgment within the American system of higher education apparently raised serious questions

---

[3] *The Purposes and Performance of Higher Education in the United States Approaching the Year 2000,* A Report and Recommendations by the Carnegie Commission on Higher Education (New York: McGraw-Hill, 1973), p. 1.

concerning the credibility of colleges and universities in general as social critics or leaders in society's self-renewal.

Faculty Role Vital

In the continuing absence of any clear voice of leadership from the academic world, church-related colleges which are courageous enough to assert without apology the importance of values education may be standing today before their greatest opportunity to open new pathways in combating cultural secularism. One of the most crucial steps for colleges which desire to follow such new pathways is to take care that a preponderance of the new faculty members whom they recruit not only display sensitivity to values and goals which stem from the Christian faith but are personally committed to them.

Colleges Perform Expanded Services

If a church-related college is institutionally committed to such values and has a faculty which shares its commitment, it will be in a position to lift a prophetic voice in the society on behalf of those values which are threatened by secularism. It is in a particularly strategic position to do this because as an institution of higher education, it works with people who will ultimately occupy positions of influence in shaping the character, establishing the policies, and setting the values of society as a whole. Moreover, in a time when the voice of the church is not heeded in public affairs as it once was, its colleges, as educational institutions, can be its spokesmen in such settings and thereby serve as an effective means of access for the church to the secular world.

At the same time the colleges need to develop and sponsor a vigorous and ongoing internal dialogue between theology and other academic disciplines. Such dialogue not only enriches the academic community, but may also serve to enrich, refresh and stimulate the church in its thinking, speaking and serving, and enlarge the effectiveness of the church's witness in the midst of a secular world.

Recent studies have indicated that church-related colleges are no longer looked upon, even by their sponsoring churches, primarily as sources for the development of lay and professional church leaders.[4] State supported colleges and universities, with their low tuition costs, are contributing larger numbers of seminary candidates than in earlier times. It would be a serious mistake for churches to interpret this trend as an evidence of a declining need for church-related colleges in the ministry of the church.

The churches should rather increase their efforts to encourage their young people who are interested in professional service in the church to enroll in church-related schools. But beyond this, the colleges ought to be seen as important instruments for preparing men and women who are motivated and equipped to be responsible citizens in the entire spectrum of occupations and professions necessary to society's well-being. This is a far more comprehensive mission than the parochial task of staffing the church.

Christians Called to Wider Commitment

One of the most compelling new pathways for colleges in contending against the force of secularism in society is suggested by Luther's understanding of Christian vocation, or calling. For a Christian, according to Luther, there can be only one vocation *(vocatio)* or calling, namely, the call of the Holy Spirit to be a child of God. Since Luther believed this call to be extended in baptism, he saw the entire life of the Christian as a grateful response to that call. Whether in work or play, study or recreation, all of life is spent in the fulfillment of that vocation as a child of God.

Every honorable profession or occupation is therefore understood to be a channel for a Christian man or woman to offer grateful service to God and to the human family. As institutions engaged in preparing young persons for a wide variety of occupations and professions, the colleges of the church have a unique opportunity to place such preparation in the highest possible context.

Students Become Key to the Future

Martin Marty has reminded us that in the recent efforts on the part of

---

[4]Richard W. Solberg, *How Church-Related Are Church-Related Colleges?* (Philadelphia: Board of Publication, Lutheran Church in America, 1980).

church-related colleges to revitalize their relationships with their churches, concern has been expressed about such key groups in the life of the colleges as trustees, faculty, and administrative leaders, and also pastors and members of congregations.[5] But he points out that the students are the group which, if captured, could revitalize both the colleges and the churches. As historical evidence, he cites two of the most vigorous missionary initiatives in American history, the Williams College movement in the early 19th century and the Student Volunteer Movement led by John R. Mott at the turn of the 20th century. The implication of his observations is that if student groups, even small ones, could be ignited on church-related campuses with similar visions of a mission in society, the seeds of something more challenging to the dominant secularism of our society than another conference of college presidents and church executives might be planted. And in time the secularized world might hear lively challenges rather than plaintive voices of frustration.

The resources for such appeals to students are intrinsic in the Christian view of the world and of God. They constitute the distinctive treasure of the church-related college if faculty and administrative leadership can articulate them and implement them through curriculum and campus life. The alternatives are a parochialism which abandons opportunity for effective witness and seeks shelter from secularism, rather than confrontation with it; or institutional capitulation to the patterns of the age, with a consequent loss of identity and of any good reason for survival. The new pathways we seek may not be new at all, but rather the reclamation of opportunities too long left unused.

[5]Marty, pp. 313 ff.

IV. New Pathways

Challenges to Freedom

Dallin H. Oaks

I t is heartening that relations within our numbers have never been better. More than a decade ago, church-related colleges and universities regarded one another suspiciously across denominational and doctrinal lines. Now, in response to the alarming deterioration in our common external environment, we draw closer to one another and unite in fellowship and support for all who believe in the existence of God, in mankind's accountability to Him, and in the appropriateness of tax exemptions for religious activities and legal protection for the teaching of moral values. More than ever we are conscious that the things that unite us are far more significant than those that divide.

Paradoxical Union in Defense of Pluralism

It is ironic but true that we must be unified to protect American heritage. Many parts of our nation were settled by immigrants trying to find a better life: Puritans, French Huguenots, German Lutherans, Baptists, Catholics, Quakers, Jews, and Mormons, to name only a few.[1]

---

[1]*Immigration and the American Tradition*, pp. xxi-xxiii (M. Rischin, ed., 1976); Lawrence G. Brown, *Immigration: Cultural Conflicts and Social Adjustments*, pp.33-39 (1969).

For many,the most important ingredient of a better life was the right to deviate from the norms prescribed by the sovereign or society in their former home. Constitutional principles guaranteeing a free exercise of religion and forbidding an official establishment were intended to provide sanctuary for religious differences such as those that distinguished these groups.

Educational institutions founded by or for the benefit of religious groups perpetuated the differences they held precious. But these institutions also embodied other, more common, values in the American heritage. In this unifying role, education has acted as the mortar that binds the mosaic of our pluralistic society. Church-related education embodies both the diversity that gives variety to our pluralistic society and the common values that unite us. If we had only diversity, our social mosaic, lacking adhesive, would be a shambles of shifting fragments. But if we yield too much to uniformity, as we tend to do when an increasing percentage of our gross national product is managed by a government that is less and less willing to tolerate differences, our educational sector and ultimately our entire society will be homogenized—drab as mortar, and uniform as a military camp.

Pressures Against Diversity

It is increasingly difficult to maintain an independent estate because the traditional sources of differentiation in higher education are disappearing,[2] casualties of strong economic, social, and legal forces that eliminate the weak, compel uniformity, and enforce equality. Small institutions are disappearing because they cannot survive the economic pressures that bear more heavily on the small. Sectarian institutions are under greater financial pressure, in part because of the legal disabilities pronounced upon the "pervasively sectarian." Single-sex institutions at the graduate level have been decreed out of existence by the Department of Health, Education and Welfare's Title IX regulations, which forbid sex discrimination in admissions, even in independent colleges.[3] Black colleges,which provided the initial educational impetus for the Civil Rights

---

[2]"The Homogenization of Higher Education," ch. 4, pp. 12-16, in *Report on Higher Education* (Frank Newman, Chairman, U. S. Govt. Printing Office, 1971).

[3]*Federal Register*, vol. 40, No. 108, June 4, 1975, Part 86, Secs. 86.15 (d), 86.21.

movement, are now threatened with extinction by the effects of government non-discrimination requirements and financial pressures.[4]

As independent church-related institutions, our greatest competitive advantage is our diversity. Independent institutions must be in a position to offer something their constituencies see as different and better than public institutions. If our right to pursue a different course in matters such as admissions, employment, and other educational policies is abridged in any way, this will further inhibit our ability to compete in and survive our current precarious financial position.

Government Challenge to Freedom

Our educational diversity—with all of its inefficiencies and even with its occasional unresponsiveness to government initiatives and worthy social action programs—is an essential ingredient for our free society. As the National Commission on Methodist Higher Education observed, "The special contributions of independent colleges and universities depend in large measure on their ability to operate as autonomous institutions, subject to a minimum of government control." Yet, as the Commission noted, "There is a danger that federal and state regulation may go so far as to deprive those institutions of the freedom and flexibility needed to perform their missions properly."[5] The greatest challenge to our freedom in Christian higher education is homogenization by government regulation.

Government regulation of higher education is basically of two types.[6] The first type is an exercise of government regulatory power that reaches colleges and universities just as it reaches other businesses. In some respects an educational institution can properly be treated like other employers. So it is that the government lumps educational institutions with factories and other employers for purposes of assuring employees a

---

[4]E.g., "Private Black Colleges See Threat in Federal Actions," *Chronicle of Higher Education*, June 26, 1978, p. 1.

[5]National Commission on United Methodist Higher Education, *Endangered Service: Independent Colleges, Public Policy and the First Amendment*, p. 88 (1976).

[6]See, generally, Dallin H. Oaks, "Government Regulation of Higher Education," an address before the Pennsylvania Association of Colleges and Universities, Sept. 25, 1978, *Vital Speeches*, Nov. 1, 1978, p. 34.

safe place to work and a financially secure savings and pension fund. Higher education is not likely to secure an exemption from the social security laws, the unemployment compensation laws, the pension reform laws, or the occupational safety and health laws simply by saying that "education is different." It *is* different, but not for this purpose.

On the other hand, some laws applicable to businesses generally, like the labor laws, should *not* be applied to education because the selection and supervision of personnel is fundamental to the mission of education, and is therefore protected by constitutional rights not applicable to businesses generally. That is why the Supreme Court rejected the National Labor Relations Board's effort to exercise jurisdiction over lay employees in high schools administered by the Catholic Bishop of Chicago. Recognizing "the critical and unique role of the teacher in fulfilling the mission of a church-operated school," the Supreme Court concluded that the exercise of N.L.R.B. jurisdiction presented "a significant risk that the First Amendment will be infringed."[7]

Danger of Control by Allocation of Funds

The second type of regulation is imposed upon higher education institutions because they are the recipients of federal financial assistance. This is the regulatory pattern under Title IX of the Education Amendments of 1972, in the Rehabilitation Act of 1973, in the so-called Buckley Amendment, and in affirmative action programs under Executive Order 11246. Here government uses its spending power to purchase conduct it has no power to compel. Specifically, it attempts to regulate higher education by conditioning some tax-supported benefit, such as categorical assistance or student eligibility for grants or loans, on a college's foregoing some immunity or subjecting itself to some regulation the government could not impose directly.

By this means, as University of Chicago President John T. Wilson has noted, "Government is using its spending power to attempt to prescribe educational policies and practices—including admissions policies, the nature of curricula and the composition of faculty." Such actions, he

---

[7]*National Labor Relations Board v. Catholic Bishop of Chicago,* 440 U.S. 490, 502 (1979).

contended, "tend to render colleges and universities in this country for the first time direct agents of social and political change."[8]

Vulnerability of Church-Related Institutions

Regulations based on the spending power and conditioned on the receipt of some government benefit are most to be feared by independent and especially church-related institutions. They jeopardize our existence on the one hand and our vital uniqueness on the other, threatening us with financial failure if we do not comply and with homogenization or secularization if we do.

Because there are serious doubts about the legality of such conditioning, this type of government regulatory effort is sure to be challenged more frequently in years to come. As one writer has noted, if we do not insist on limits on the government's power to place conditions on the funds it allocates, the government could make a complete mockery of the restrictions the constitution imposes on its enumerated legislative powers, abrogating both the tenth amendment reservation of powers to the states and the people and the due process clause's protection against arbitrary governmental action.[9] This is the area of greatest sensitivity in government regulation of higher education, and this is the area where educational institutions should concentrate their greatest efforts in seeking freedom from government regulation.

Independent higher education of course takes no exception to regulations requiring accountability. We should insure that government funds are expended for the purposes for which they are provided and that they are not expended in ways that run directly counter to legitimate government objectives, such as by discrimination in the use of government financed property and facilities.

---

[8]John T. Wilson, "The Threat to Private Colleges," *Christian Science Monitor*, June 20, 1978.

[9]"The Federal Conditional Spending Power: A Search for Limits," 70 *Northwestern University Law Review* 293, 330 (1975); Philip A. Lacovara, "How Far Can the Federal Camel Slip Under the Academic Tent?" 4 *Journal of College and University Law*, 223 (1977).

Distinction Between Public and Independent

But the principle of accountability should not be extended to make an entire institution and all of its programs accountable for compliance with government policies that Congress made applicable only to the specific program or activity receiving federal financial assistance.[10] Such an extension would quickly erase a major distinction between public and independent, seriously undercutting the vital freedom and diversity of independent higher education. We must insist that accountability regulations are always "program-specific," which means that they do not extend regulatory authority over an entire institution on the basis of the receipt of federal financial assistance by one of its programs or activities, as the Title IX regulations attempt to do. Similarly, we must insist—as Grove City College is attempting to establish in its vitally important litigation— that government regulation of an institution not be based on the receipt of financial assistance by its students. The role of government is so pervasive in our society that every social institution and every program or activity is affected by it. If we do not limit government regulation to what is directly supported, there will be no autonomous field of action remaining for private or independent institutions.

Vital Importance of Right to Religious Preference

If we are to accomplish our unique educational objectives, church-related institutions must be able to exercise the broadest range of freedom in admissions, employment, curriculum and research. The right to pursue distinctive policies in the hiring and direction of faculty is particularly vital. In their notable study, *Government Regulation of Religiously Affiliated Higher Education*, Philip R. Moots and Edward M. Gaffney, Jr. report that 84 percent of the 220 religiously affiliated colleges who responded to their survey exercised a religious preference in the selection

---

[10]Dallin H. Oaks, "Title IX: Administrative, Legal, and Constitutional Aspects," an address before the Western College Association, March 10, 1977, 5 *Utah Bar Journal* 3 (1977) and *Vital Speeches*, Vol. 23, No. 12, Apr. 1, 1977, pp. 372-76; "HEW's Regulation Under Title IX of the Education Amendments of 1972: Ultra Vires Challenges," 1976 *BYU Law Review* 132; "Title IX Sex Discrimination Regulations: Impact on Private Education," 65 *Kentucky Law Journal* 656 (1977).

of at least some of their faculty, and many others—though less than a majority—considered religious belief or practice in the hiring of all employees.[11] Representatives of Lutheran St. Olaf's College and Catholic Notre Dame University gave the same explanation of the need for a religious preference in hiring policies:

> "All the programs and money in the world cannot help us achieve our stated ideals [at St. Olaf's College] unless most of our faculty and Administration embrace them out of conviction. . . . [We] try to hire the most capable. . . but we hire only those who convince us that they believe in our distinctness as a college of the Church. . . ."[12]

> "If Notre Dame is to remain Catholic, the only institutional way for assuring this is to secure a faculty with prominent representation of committed and articulate believers who purposely seek the comradeship of others to weave their faith into the full fabric of their intellectual life. . . . [Notre Dame will maintain its Catholic identity by] assuring that committed Catholics predominate in the community."[13]

Church-related colleges and universities obviously cannot afford to allow the vital matter of faculty selection to be directed or influenced by government bureaucrats who, as a recent editorial observed, show a "passionate attachment to simple and inappropriate numbers, and not much concern for anything else about the educational institutions" being regulated.[14]

Religion in Anti-Discrimination Formulas

The increasing inclusion of the word "religion" in anti-discrimination formulas betrays the current insensitivity to the latitude religious institutions must be able to exercise to preserve their diversity.

---

[11]Philip R. Moots and Edward McGlynn Gaffney, Jr., "Government Regulation of Religiously Affiliated Higher Education," ch. 2, pp. 3-4 (A Study for the Sloan Commission on Government and Higher Education, 1979).

[12]*Id.*, at ch. 2, p. 8.

[13]*Ibid.*

[14]"Waiting for H.E.W.," *Wall Street Journal*, Feb. 7, 1978, p. 14, col. 1.

Prohibitions against discrimination on the basis of religion are appropriate as to public institutions. It would be unconstitutional for a state institution to consider religion in its hiring or promotion. Our Constitution commits us against a religious test for public employment.[15] But when a church sponsors and supports a college or university, it should surely have the right to consider the religious belief or practice of the students it admits and those it employs to achieve its institutional objectives. The amended Civil Rights Act grants that privilege as to employment,[16] but some government agencies and private groups, including some accrediting bodies, persist in challenging religious discrimination as if it were to be judged by the same public policies and legal and moral standards that forbid racial discrimination.

The establishment of a new Department of Education is also a cause for concern among many educators. Armed with a concentration of regulatory powers over higher education, a federal Department of Education will have an irresistible tendency to exercise them over the private sector. The bureaucracy is likely to have the same tendency as the small boy who is given a hammer and promptly finds that "everything he encounters needs pounding."[17] The tendency toward increased regulation by a new department is especially concerning in view of its proponents' argument that the new department will give us greater efficiency in government. This threatens to remove one of the last defenses of those who resist increasing government direction of higher education—the government's inefficiency! We have all taken comfort in the taxpayer's wry observation that "we're just lucky we're not gettin' all the government we're payin' for." The regulation of education is one area where we don't want our money's worth!

Seven-Step Program

So what is to be done? I suggest the following seven-step program for

---

[15]United States Constitution, Article VI; *Torcaso v. Watkins*, 367 U.S. 488 (1961).

[16]42 U.S.C. § 2000e-2(e). Also see Office of Federal Contract Compliance Final Regulations, 40 *Fed. Reg.* 13218 (March 25, 1975).

[17]Paul Dickson, "Rules to Rue," *Mainliner Magazine*, Dec. 1978, p. 52.

the survival of independent and especially church-related higher education.[18]

(1)   Independent higher education must regulate itself, to identify and eliminate abuses that would otherwise be used to justify government regulation.

(2)   We must work to perpetuate and increase legal incentives for charitable giving to educational institutions, restoring the significance of the charitable deduction in addition to the so-called standard deduction.

(3)   We must resist any attempts to predicate government regulation on the benefits that flow to educational institutions and other recipients of charitable gifts. If the recipient of a charitable gift is thereby subjected to regulation, we have lost the independent financial support that is essential to our survival, or else we have become subject to the same regulations as public institutions, thus destroying the autonomy that justifies our existence and allows us to accomplish our mission.

(4)   We should prefer government assistance to higher education that is indirect, such as grants or loans to students. This will minimize the prospects of government regulation and at the same time preserve the option of indirect government assistance for the numerous independent institutions that cannot survive without it.

(5)   We should seek to have laws and regulations affecting higher education drafted to incorporate three important but not yet established distinctions:

> *First*, because of the First Amendment freedoms that should be enjoyed by educational institutions, lawmakers and regulation writers should *exclude education* from certain rules that are generally applicable to other organizations.

> *Second*, lawmakers and regulation writers should *exempt independent educational institutions* from some of the body of rules otherwise generally applicable to public institutions. Specifically, the extent of regulation should bear some relationship to the magnitude of government financial assistance involved, and it should not be premised on assistance received by students.

---

[18]This program is described at greater length in Oaks, n. 6, *supra*.

Third, from the laws and regulations otherwise appropriate for independent colleges and universities, rule-makers should carve out appropriate *exceptions to accommodate* the special constitutional freedoms guaranteed to *church-related institutions.*

(6)   Lawmakers and regulation writers should take account of the different nature of the discriminations they outlaw, and be more discriminating in their anti-discrimination. For example, a law or regulation forbidding *racial* discrimination is not necessarily sound and workable when applied across the board in outlawing discrimination on the basis of *sex* or *religion*. In some instances, the sexes need to be treated differently to serve important values of health, safety, morals, and the free exercise of religion, and in all instances religion is a constitutionally protected consideration that must receive the special consideration it is denied by automatically lumping it with other bases of discrimination.

(7)   Church-related colleges and universities need to band together to lobby against unsound and unworkable laws and regulations, and where illegal laws or regulations have been enacted, to challenge them in court. Since regulatory initiatives are rarely reversible, we must lose no time in trying to stem the tide. This must be done if the independent—and especially the church-related—sector is to preserve the autonomy necessary for each institution to fulfill its unique mission.

The price is high, but it must be paid if we are to preserve our freedom to practice the diversities by which we serve. We cannot accomplish our mission as church-related colleges and universities if our educational lights are even partly obscured by government regulation. We must be free to witness and practice our religious heritage and values by teaching spiritual *and* secular knowledge and by working to bring those teachings into harmony in the lives of men and women to prepare them for a balanced and full life of service to God and fellowmen. May God help us in this sacred mission.

V.   New Pathways

The Church-Related College
and the Preservation of Pluralism

James S. Barrett

C ontemporary American higher education is a dual system, in part publicly supported and governed and in part sponsored by private organizations. This system is fairly unique in the modern world, and is reflective of the social and economic principles which American culture represents. Of all the ways of characterizing our system of higher education, perhaps the best words have been *diversity* and *mass.*[1] Sectarian, independent, church-related, experimental, large, small, public, residential, commuting, adult—these are all terms having meaning in regard to types of institutions, and there are many more. This characterizes what is meant by diversity: the presence of many different and diffuse means for delivering educational goals to the society. Some, noting this pattern from outside, have discerned notable similarities despite the apparent variety, and have concluded that common purposes, problems

---

[1]Reference for our system's uniqueness and for its characteristics of diversity and mass can be found in Joseph Ben-David, *American Higher Education* (New York: McGraw-Hill, 1972), Chapter One; and Sir Eric Ashby, *Any Person, Any Study* (New York: McGraw-Hill, 1970); Jacques Barzun, *The American University* (New York: Harper & Row, 1968), p. 1.

and experiences exist.[2] This is undoubtedly true, for without essential commonality having as its aim useful attainments, society could not and would not support such diversity. Admission of similar general goals, however, does not necessarily mean adoption of similar means for achievement nor of similar priorities among all the appropriate goals. Just as all persons are simultaneously alike yet different, so are human institutions diverse while generally similar. In a society based on competition and capitalism this diverse approach to common goals is not only likely, but expected.

Mass is another term characterizing American higher education, for another social factor—a strong belief in individualism and equality of opportunity—has propelled our educational system toward service to all citizens who can profit from it. Catering to the economies of scale involved in mass education has created problems, not the least of which has been the fact that all citizens are not equally treated in daily life; thus some have not been in a position to profit from higher education. Equality is an ideal rather than a fact itself, and working out what is meant by the term has proven frustrating and occasionally dangerous. Most observers do agree that remarkable progress has been made, nonetheless, and that American higher education is about the only system on earth that approaches true mass opportunity.[3] It is apparent that mass education and educational diversity go hand in hand, and that each has been in support of the other. This is because diverse people, beliefs, needs, and priorities can be handled together only if the system is flexible enough to permit widely varying institutional responses to coexist. Not everyone can or should be treated identically, and therefore diversity is necessary if such a mass effort as the education of the public is to succeed. When the society values freedom and individuality as much as equality, the need for diversity becomes not merely logically required, but morally imperative.

Justifying Private Higher Education

If diversity is a key element in modern American higher education, and the independent sector is a component of that diversity, how do we connect

---

[2]Ben-David, Chapter One.

[3]Ben-David, Chapter One, pp. 1-5; Ashby; any number of other works, speeches, etc.

the two in such a way as to justify private higher education? Surely diversity is no monopoly of private institutions.[4] We have only to note the incredible variety of public institutions to admit this. Nor, for that matter, can the mere distinction of private versus public help us. Those acquainted with the history of American higher education know that private institutions have always acknowledged, and had acknowledged for them, a public trust.[5] The *Dartmouth College* case established that a private institution is free from state control in spite of its provision of a public service—education—rather than because of it. Corporate control and ownership of property was the issue, not education *per se.*[6] In the early nineteenth century public support for private institutions was widely accepted and acknowledged. Only when sectarian considerations and the mushrooming number of private colleges outstripped the ability of public largess to aid them did private sources of funding and sponsorship assume major importance.[7] Today, over a century later, the ability of private sources to assist private institutions is being outstripped, and the state is increasingly being asked to help—again. Many educators, being unaware of this historical pattern, have assumed that private status has always meant financial independence from public monies and influence. What is true is that public support for private higher education has always existed.

---

[4]Any summary of reports, such as the Carnegie series or state comprehensive plans for postsecondary education, will demonstrate the extraordinary diversity of public institutions. An example is the fact that V.M.I., the University of California, the University of the State of New York—Regents Degree Program, Northern Virginia Community College, and the Colorado School of Mines are all public institutions.

[5]This concept is established in most educational philosophy. For reference see John Henry Cardinal Newman, *The Idea of a University* (London: Longmans, 1927, new edition), the preface and introductory remarks, pp. i-xxii and 1-18; National Commission on United Methodist Higher Education, *Endangered Service* (Nashville: 1976), p. 23; Barzun, Chapter One, pp. 10-33. Even Robert Maynard Hutchins, *The Higher Learning in America* (New Haven: Yale, 1974, 17th edition), makes oblique reference to it in Chapter One, External Conditions.

[6]*Trustees of Dartmouth College v. Woodward,* 17 U.S. (4 Wheat.) 518, 4 L. Ed. 629 (1819).

[7]See Frederick Rudolph, *The American College and University* (New York: Random House, 1962), 185-190. The myth of private status arose largely to defend the (then) new appeals to private donors and benefactors in the retrenchment years prior to the Civil War.

Private status means private control, not totally private support. Here we must return to *Dartmouth* and to the historic public-private relationship, for if the difference is based on the concept of control, then this implies that the rationale for private higher education is not economic, either.

Economic Rationale Insufficient

Before taking up the question posed by the word *control,* it is well to consider further the economic implications of private status. One of the current arguments advanced to defend private higher education has been that its existence saves the taxpayer money.[8] This is accomplished by obviating the necessity of providing public classroom space for students served in private institutions. There is little doubt that this is true if one considers that, given mass opportunity, everyone now enrolled in private institutions would have to be accommodated somehow if these institutions ceased to exist. "Somehow" would necessarily mean expanded—in some cases upgraded—public facilities. However, if by saving taxpayer dollars one means that the private institutions take care of themselves, then this rationale must be severely qualified. First, any taxpayer who pays private tuition knows that he pays double: once to support the system he does not use, and again to support the one he does. Second, whenever circumstances induce or compel the private sector to seek public relief, such as tuition vouchers, the result is to end significant economic segregation between the two parts of the system. As a result of these observations one must conclude that the economic rationale, while valid, cannot stand alone as a sufficient argument in favor of private higher education. If we accept Rudolph and other historical observers, the fact is that the sheer economics of the situation did not inspire the private sector in the first place.[9] Private schools did not arise due to economic impulses requiring private as opposed to public education; the private economic

---

[8]As an example see the arguments presented in *Endangered Service,* pp. 28-34. The weakness of this position for defending private education is pointed out in Paul Woodring, *The Higher Learning in America: A Reassessment* (New York: McGraw-Hill, 1968), pp. 7-8.

[9]As other observers one could cite Cardinal Newman, the preface; David D. Henry, *Challenges Past, Challenges Present* (San Francisco: Jossey-Bass, 1975), preface and pp. 4-7.

concept instead followed the formation of the institutions. All segments of society founded institutions at one time or another, and the idea of "private" institutions, in regard to their financing, is largely a myth. This discourse gets us back, then, to what did inspire private institutions—control.

Control Accomplishes Purpose

Many students of American higher education, notably Rudolph, Ben-David and Veysey (and indeed, students of higher education in general, notably Cardinal Newman) have observed that religious impulses inspired the creation of the system of higher education.[10] Since the early days of theological education, other social institutions have established educational centers. These include all or nearly all religious denominations and sects, to train lay persons as well as clerics; utopian societies, to experiment with new educational approaches; private groups and municipal organizations, to provide needed local talent; and the state, to provide public officers and to respond to public demands for education by groups unable to provide it for themselves. In each of these instances, and in the many others that could be cited, the central ingredient inspiring the establishment of educational institutions has been some purpose. Mission, goals, aims—these have been the backbone of the American system of higher education. People do not sacrifice, save, campaign, or raise taxes without a reason. Educationally, the reason should be that some group or interest is served better by providing such a facility than by not doing so. In our particular, this requires two things: belief in the value of higher education; and proof that it does make a difference.[11] Here we at last locate the reason why control is so central to rationalizing higher education in a free, competitive system. Since a belief operationalized into a set of goals is necessary to galvanize the founding of an institution, it follows that without effective control that set of goals cannot be realized. Without

---

[10]This has all been cited above with the exception of Laurence R. Veysey, *The Emergence of the American University* (Chicago: University of Chicago, 1965) pp. 1-56; and Ben-David, pp. 11-13 and 52-56.

[11]The emergence of a pragmatic defense of higher education—that it indeed does make a difference, occurred from 1860 through the 1930's. For this see Veysey, pp. 57-120; Henry, p. 5.

control, ownership is meaningless. And that is precisely the point Justice Marshall makes in *Dartmouth College.*

Purpose Crucial

In regard to private higher education, then, control is important because it permits special purposes to be accomplished. This is true for public institutions as well, since they too have purposes and must be effectively controlled in order to fulfill them. We have seen, though, that it is difficult to define *private* as a term, as long as one tries to do this via economic and legal means. *Private* becomes a vital term, however, as soon as it is realized that it means all institutions *not public;* i.e., all those whose purposes and thus the aims of their founders differ in some significant aspect from the purposes and hence accountability of state-controlled institutions. The importance of the private sector to American higher education is primarily its role in supporting diversity of purpose, of providing alternative structures, priority rankings, and strategies for accomplishing educational aims. Diversity does not mean mere physical differences; it means diverse ideas, approaches and results. Diversity is pluralism in its most meaningful form, since a complex society permits no less.[12] Diversity promotes stability by permitting the forces of competition to eliminate real aberrations while preserving valid alternatives which challenge and reinforce each other.[13] In addition, diversity makes a demand. It requires that diverse institutions have a reason for their existence, that a genuine purpose remains alive and that diversity does not degenerate into its own purpose. This is why materialistic arguments for private higher education are totally incomplete. If the only rationale is to be "private"—whatever that means—then nothing has been demonstrated justifying independence from public control.[14] The state system is quite

---

[12]These ideas are developed most strongly in Morris T. Keeton, *Models and Mavericks* (New York: McGraw-Hill, 1971), pp. vii (by Clark Kerr) and 1-2; *Endangered Service,* pp. 23-45; Woodring, p. 15 and 215-220; Andrew M. Greeley, *From Backwater to Mainstream* (New York: McGraw-Hill, 1969), pp. 158-163.

[13]Jack Hirschleifer, "A Dangerous Precedent," in Sidney Hook, Paul Kurtz & Miro Todorovich, eds., *The Idea of a Modern University* (Buffalo: Prometheus, 1974),pp. 251-252.

[14]See Barzun, pp. 240-242, 285.

diverse, and since all education has a public impact, non-public institutions without a genuine *raison d'être* will be hard-pressed to argue why they should not be accountable to public agents.[15] It is for these very critical reasons that institutions with sound goals and purposes need not panic at the state of contemporary higher education. Historically private higher education has always scrambled for financial support, and times have been endured in past generations equal in hardship to the present. One need only mention the Civil War, or the depressions that followed it, to illustrate the point.[16] Examination of these times also shows that nearly every device now in use to avoid financial embarrassment has been tried before.[17] In the process, some rather gimmicky and unsavory tactics and shibboleths have been raised to the status of rationales. The idea that educational quality is unrelated to salaries paid staff members, that hallowed traditions produce superior alumni, that intimate atmospheres are crucial to education, and that low faculty-student ratios promote learning have all been invoked, and none of them has convinced, and rightly not.[18] Another idea is to criticize public institutions for their lack of academic freedom due to political constraints. This would have merit were it not implied thereby that the private institutions are immune from such transgressions. In fact, all institutions are subordinate to the purposes of their controllers, and provincial or parochial dominance can be just as stultifying as the state, or as liberating, depending upon leadership and external circumstances.[19] Another reaction to the present stress has been to change the nature of private institutions, to make them "relevant" to the present student marketplace. This process is good if indeed a specific institution needs to redefine its purpose in light of modern ideas on education. Generally, however, this has produced a switching from a liber-

---

[15]As a warning on this matter, which will be repeated later on, see *Runyon v. McCrary*, 427 U.S. 160, 96 S.C. + 2586, 49 L. Ed. 2d 415 (1976), where the court held a federal statute prohibiting racial discrimination in school admissions applicable to a private institution on the theory of contract.

[16]See Rudolph, pp. 221-240; Henry, pp. 1-37.

[17]Rudolph, pp. 191-915.

[18]Woodring, p. 14.

[19]*Ibid.*

al arts curriculum to a vocational curriculum.[20] In addition to the near-impossibility of achieving high-quality professional training at such institutions without expensive additions, there is the fact that this directly competes with the licensing responsibility of the state. Since the first responsibility of the state is to those practical concerns essential for social survival, it follows that public institutions are equipped and oriented to professional and vocational goals. Primarily non-professional private institutions surrender a large part of their purpose (and rationale) when they mimic an already existing system.[21] Vocational consciousness has come about as a result of general economic decline—there is good reason to believe it represents a safety-valve reaction rather than a change of cultural values. The meaning of the liberal arts may change, but the requirements of graduate and professional schools show no readiness (nor does business or government) to adopt expectations other than facility with language, skill in quantitative methods, logical reasoning, and awareness of the whys, whats and hows of our culture.

Maintaining Purpose During Periods of Stress

The above pitfall catalog in private realization is not meant to apply universally or to ignore real currents in history. It simply reinforces the need to adopt and maintain educationally valuable purposes for educational institutions, and not to depend upon economics, society, or political ideas to fill a vacuum. Our society is not static. It is changing all the time, and private institutions must respond to this.[22] But even when change occurs in institutions, it must bring with it a new purpose that

---

[20]See the observations in works such as C. Arnold Anderson, Mary Jean Bowman and Vincent Tinto, *Where Colleges Are and Who Attends* (New York: McGraw-Hill, 1972); Philip C. Ritterbush, ed., *Let the Entire Community Become Our University* (Washington: Acropolis, 1972); Dyckman W. Vermilye, ed., *Relating Work and Education* (San Francisco: Jossey-Bass, 1977); Carnegie Commission on Higher Education, *College Graduates and Jobs* (New York: McGraw-Hill, 1973); and the observations of outsiders such as Ashby and Ben-David.

[21]Woodring, pp. 14-15; Paul Kurtz, "Excellence and Irrelevance, in Hook *et al.,* pp. 185-201; Arthur Bestor, "Reinforcing the Challenge," in the same the volume, *passim.*

[22]Samuel Lubell, "Counsel for the Future," in Hook, *et al.,* pp. 266-267.

adequately defends independence and its place in diversity.[23] Precisely because of diversity this is a duty that each private institution must accomplish individually. For this reason a decline in enrollment in viable institutions is not cause for concern unless it reveals a pattern threatening to all. Institutions without support or purpose cannot exist, and quite probably should not as well. At present there are forces at work which threaten private higher education and these deserve notice.

The cost of education is the universal problem of higher education today, and it has brought with it a greater problem. In order to achieve a support level that maintains viability, private institutions have sought public funding, since private sources no longer—in most cases—supply enough support. This strategy has brought with it some threat of loss of control, since the state asserts its right to exercise influence as a price of such support (remember *Dartmouth College*). Governmental regulation, especially affirmative action, is a crucial subject these days. [24] Times are also different from the early nineteenth century—today public responsibility for education is taken for granted—and the climate makes it difficult for institutions to resist public priorities while accepting public support. Private higher education, therefore, must respond to two queries: is it important enough to support in hard times; and is it important enough in a non-material sense to support without imposing onerous conditions that may effectively end its independence? Economic arguments help answer the first question. Yes, the private sector is large enough to severely cripple educational policy and planning were it to collapse.[25] The other

---

[23]Barzun, p. 285; NCOUMHE, *Toward 2000* (Nashville: 1976), p. 56; another example comes from Jane E. Smith Browning and John B. Williams, "History and Goals of Black Institutions of Higher Learning;" and Gregory Kannerstein, "Black Colleges: Self-Concept," both in Charles V. Willie and Roland R. Edmonds, eds., *Black Colleges in America* (New York: Teachers College, 1978) pp. 68-96 and 29-50.

[24]See Hirschleifer, p. 251; any number of observations on state-institutional relations. Virtually any contemporary periodical, journal or book will have a reference to this crisis.

[25]See *Endangered Service* and reports such as Howard R. Bowen and W. John Minter, *Private Higher Education, 1976* (Washington: Association of American Colleges, 1976). One can also cite the disproportionate influence of private institutions on producing America's leaders: see Robert H. Knapp, *The Origins of*

question is more complex. We might start to consider it by remembering two old adages: "Relevance is in the eye of the beholder;" and "There is nothing that clarifies the mind so much as the approach of the hangman's noose."[26] These mean, in rough application to this discourse, that one must be true to one's own purpose in order to expect the same of anyone else; and that exigency often has the effect of causing the reassessment of purpose.

Private higher education must have purpose to be viable. This may be faith, hypothesis, or any number of other inspirations, but it must exist and justify the institution's existence. Rapid abandonment of purpose in panic may cause society to devalue the private sector, and it may also reveal that purpose was not really there to begin with. [27] Church colleges that scramble to redefine their mission and governance in order to receive public money do not demonstrate allegiance to purpose; neither do private universities that cater to the immediate whims of donors or government agencies. If the private sector in higher education is valuable, it will survive and enjoy public support without surrendering that which rationalizes its existence. There is another side as well: private institutions cannot deviate too far from socially acceptable values without expecting decline in support and the imposition of requirements for regaining that support. For instance, if it is obvious to all that neither public nor private higher education has historically provided opportunity for minorities, and the mood of society is that they should begin to do so, then it is pointless for private institutions guilty of this historic pattern to cry "foul" when they attempt simultaneously to receive public money and avoid public responsibility.[28] Much of the disorganization in the private response to governmental conditions is undoubtedly due to awareness of the above point. How can

---

American Humanistic Scholars (Englewood Cliffs: Prentice-Hall, 1964), and Cedric A. Larson, *Who's Who: Sixty Years of American Eminence* (New York: McDowell, 1958), pp. 239-258.

[26]First quotation from Bestor, p. 261; second from Isadore Blumen, "The Need for Coalition and Proper Strategy" in Hook, *et al.*, p. 266.

[27]Warnings to this effect are legion. Some of the better examples include Benjamin E. Mays, "The Black College in Higher Education," Willie & Edmonds, pp. 19-28; Greeley, pp. 72-84; Cardinal Newman, preface and introduction; and Hutchins, *The Higher Learning.*

[28]Remember *Runyon v. McCrary.* The market works both ways.

any institution claim to be publicly important yet completely above public accountability? Thus we see that private higher education is not now, nor ever has been, completely independent. Neither the state nor the individual is above the laws or mores of society. Control remains in private hands, *ceteris paribus.* Nor would any of us, if we thought about it, wish a real establishment of privilege whereby no accountability exists. Genuine state interference in private higher education will be limited by political and social forces so long as diversity remains important to Americans. On the other hand, the existence of socially aberrant institutions will be limited by these same forces. We must work for this balance to continue, both by reaffirming the worth of private higher education *and* by working to insure that it responds to the best interests of American society.

Private higher education is an alternative to public higher education. It serves needs the state cannot meet, such as religious training, and it can experiment in ways the state cannot easily match; witness the plethora of curricular and community living innovations pioneered at private colleges. Morris Keeton's title, *Models and Mavericks*, in the Carnegie series is an apt summation of what private higher education can and should be.[29] Practical arguments aside (while recognizing their worth), it is the purposeful pursuit of excellence in the spirit of competition and pluralism that distinguishes and justifies the private sector. Come to think of it, that is not such an impractical rationale after all. We might end by reflecting on Cardinal Newman's quotation of Macaulay: "When we reflect on the tremendous assaults she has survived, we find it difficult to conceive in what way she is to perish."[30]

---

[29]Keeton and Woodring, among others, have already been used to make these points. Other items not raised here, but worth considering, are convenience (Anderson, Bowman and Tinto), the retention rate (*Endangered Service*), and the demands of special communities (ethnic, sectarian) or the demand for excellence (*Who's Who* and Knapp).

[30]Macaulay referring to the survivability of Catholicism and quoted by Cardinal Newman, p. 438. This is a paraphrase of the remark, slightly out of context but interesting.

VI. New Pathways

The Role and Purpose
of the Institutions of the Church

Abner V. McCall

Institutions of the church are not churches but instruments of the church to carry on selected works in the world. Most such institutions are separately incorporated as public eleemosynary trusts. Their funds and properties are irrevocably dedicated to public use. In most cases, trustees of Baptist institutions are elected by the sponsoring state convention, and thereafter are primarily responsible to the trust to execute the provisions of the trust. Such a trust is enforceable by the state Attorney General in the state courts. For example, a trust set up for the purpose of a hospital must operate a hospital. If legally entrusted as a college, it must operate a college. All church-sponsored institutions are tax exempt and receive gifts from the general public on the basis of this dedication to a public trust.

If an institution should attempt to operate in violation of law or, in the case of a college, reasonable rules of accreditation associations, the Attorney General or donors or beneficiaries could well challenge in court whether the trustees are properly carrying out their trust. A court could order that proper procedure be followed, or it could remove trustees. If trustees are acting pursuant to church direction in such a case, the court could terminate the power of the church to select trustees.

In a recent case the trustees of Wilson College, a small college for women in Chambersburg, Pennsylvania, after several years of declining student enrollment and deficit operation, decided to close the college and convert the remaining endowment into a scholarship fund for women students to attend other colleges. The decision of the trustees was challenged in a Pennsylvania court by some Wilson College alumni who had contributed to the college. The court issued a decree removing some of the trustees and enjoining the remaining trustees from closing the college or disposing of any of its assets without prior permission of the court. The court decision in this case, which was settled without appeal by the resignation of the trustees, illustrates that once a church-related college is established as a public trust, the donors and public in general can insist that the trustees faithfully execute the trust to operate a college.

At one time the works that church-related institutions selected to do were those which no one else would or could carry on, generally because there was no profit to be made in doing so. Thus, the church established homes for children and for the aged, hospitals, schools and colleges. These have been the traditional institutions of the Southern Baptist churches. At first the churches had almost a monopoly in operating these types of institutions. Later the state entered these fields of service, and today state homes for children and for the aged, state hospitals, and state schools and colleges far outnumber the church institutions and perform most of these beneficial services.

Institutions: A Social Implication of the Gospel

In the beginning the church founded these institutions because their services were needed by people in general. Performance of these services was an implementation of the Christian command to love thy neighbor. The institutions were a social implementation of the gospel intended to make a better society. They were witnesses for the Lord by the performance of good deeds. In the performance of the beneficial services of child care, care of the aged and infirm, hospitalization, and educational opportunities, Baptist institutions were also available to preach and teach the gospel.

Particularly the Christian college offers a happy combination of the opportunities of performing the beneficial service of secular education and of imparting understanding of Christian principles and values. Southern Baptists have tens of millions invested in their colleges, and it would be folly to abandon this investment which can yield such rich dividends in terms of providing a means of serving young people, teaching them the gospel, and strengthening their faith.

Baptist colleges, of course, have played a fundamental and supportive role in the development of the Southern Baptist Convention and its world-wide missionary enterprise. In fact, Southern Baptist colleges were founded several years before the establishment of the Southern Baptist Convention on May 18, 1845, in Augusta, Georgia. Furman was founded in 1825, Mississippi College in 1826, Georgetown College in 1829, Mercer University in 1833, Wake Forest College in 1834, and Baylor University was founded in February, 1845.

Although early Baptist colleges were established to train men for the Christian ministry, from the very start their purpose was also to make education available to all who wished it. Out of all proportion to their size and number, these colleges influenced the culture of the South through their graduates, both lay and ministerial.

While the churches supported the colleges, the colleges also in turn undergirded church growth. To quote from an article entitled, "Present at the Creation" (by Ben C. Fisher in *Collage*):

> As a matter of fact, Southern Baptists never made much progress until they began to understand and make use of institutional witness. In spite of the fact that some are saying that Baptists have never depended upon such a witness, Baptist history speaks to the contrary. The first Baptist institutions were colleges and schools; orphanages followed; then hospitals and homes for the aging. While the Baptist state papers usually began as an individual project, in a real sense they are institutional products of a denomination that early recognized the power of the printed word. Until these various institutions were established, no great church growth is to be noted.

Piety: Never a Substitute for Quality

Sometimes church-sponsored institutions have not rendered the *best* services. They have operated mediocre hospitals, homes, and schools, usually for lack of adequate resources. Sometimes, particularly in the case of schools and colleges, sponsoring bodies have placed unnecessary, narrow restrictions on the institutions and thereby caused mediocre services to be rendered. Some have sought to excuse these poor services by substituting piety. Piety in the operation of any Christian institution is good. However, piety has never been, is not now, and never will be an acceptable substitute for service of good quality. The fact that a physician is a zealous Christian does not excuse incompetent or careless health care. The fact that a college professor is the soul of piety is no excuse for incompetent or indifferent teaching. A Christian board of trustees and administrators does not excuse poor equipment and poor procedures. Because piety has sometimes been used to excuse mediocrity, secular critics often assume that piety always implies mediocrity and is a mere cover for it. Nothing could be further from the truth.

Christ inspires the best. Nothing less than the best effort is worthy of Christ. His followers should be ashamed to put His name on the second-rate, whether it is health care, child care, or education. What they do in Christ's name should be excellent. It should be attractive and winsome. Then it is truly witnessing for Christ. True piety abhors mediocrity and calls for excellence.

Some believe that in the field of education the discovered truth and the revealed truth cannot be honestly and effectively taught together—that Athens and Jerusalem cannot be combined. Some who believe this are non-believers. At the other extreme, some who believe it are fanatical and narrow believers. But the revealed truth and the discovered truth can be taught in the same institution, and both can be dealt with honestly and completely. As a matter of fact, they complement each other to produce the whole truth, and neither is complete without the other. It was Dr. Elton Trueblood who wrote of the Christian college: "Its greatness declines when it ceases to hold the love of God and the love of learning in a single context."

Five Characteristics of a Christian College

(1)   First it should be a *good* college, with a program of education that needs no apology. The trustees, administrators, faculty, and students should be competent, qualified, and dedicated to their work. They should be equal to those in any secular college, whether public or private. Just as a Christian physician, lawyer, plumber, teacher, or airline pilot should first be a good physician, lawyer, plumber, etc., so the emphasis upon

Christianity and the impact of Christianity should be over and above and in addition to the first characteristic. In addition to the usual secular motivations to succeed as a college professor, the Christian professor should have the extra motivation that he is responsible to his Lord to use his talents as a teacher to the fullest extent. Similarly the Christian student should have this extra motivation in his studies to prepare himself for service to the Lord after graduation. Christian commitment and dedication should produce excellence in performance as a teacher or a student. The church-related college must emphasize good teaching. It may encourage research and publication by the faculty but it must demand good teaching.

(2)   Most of those involved should be professed Christians—trustees, administrators, teachers, and students. It should be the policy of the college and the sponsoring denomination to appoint such trustees, administrators, and teachers and to attract such students. Of course, none will be perfect, and perfection should not be expected, but there should be a prevailing commitment to Christ. The college should be a *Christian community* as well as an academic community. It is as hard to have a good Christian community as it is to have a good academic community. Any Christian institution must constantly work at being a Christian community.

(3)   All persons involved should strive to live and carry out their duties as Christians. They should have Christian compassion and concern for each other. Administrators and teachers should strive to love each other and act accordingly. It cannot be assumed, because a teacher has a Doctor of Philosophy degree in his discipline, that he is a caring, concerned teacher. There is little or nothing in the program of graduate education in the ordinary university which teaches a person to have compassion and concern as a teacher. Students and teachers should strive to establish relationships of Christian love. At Baylor University, the president interviews every teacher who is hired. Every one of them is told that the administration, above all, expects the teacher to have respect, compassion, concern—yes, even to strive *to love* every student and to treat students accordingly. New instructors are advised that they are expected also to love their fellow teachers—and even to strive for that impossible height of loving the university administrators! All on the campus are encouraged to act toward each other in such a manner of love that the

observing world can tell that the institution is Christian. "By this," it is hoped, "shall all men know that ye are my disciples, if ye have love one to another." Such an attitude is the *sine qua non* of a Christian community— whether it is a college, hospital, children's home, or church itself. No matter what else is present, it is not Christian if Christian love is not prevalent. An administrator who is careful to hire Christians on this basis seldom has to fire anyone, but when this becomes necessary, it is usually not because of academic incompetence but for lack of Christian respect and concern for others.

(4)   The teaching of the academic courses should be done not only in the Christian manner with compassion and concern for the student, but with whatever Christian content is possible. This will vary from course to course. While there may be no Christian math or Baptist chemistry, in most courses the Christian view of truth held by the teacher will come through. In some courses, such as history, literature, sociology, philosophy, and religion, the philosophy of life of the teacher will inevitably be projected. Here, the secular and the sacred must be combined. The revealed and the discovered truth must both be examined. The professor's teaching should reveal that he believes that man is related to God and that life thereby has significance, dignity, and integrity, and more: that life is touched with eternity here and hereafter, and bears in both worlds an eternal significance.

(5)   The total program of the college will include specific programs of religious education and worship such as chapel, prayer meetings, and courses in Christianity taught by professed Christians. Programs on the campus should encourage witness and mission work. The parietal rules should reflect Christian social practices of personal discipline and morality. Christianity should be manifest on the campus, in the classroom, in the library, in a dormitory, in the gymnasium, in the social parlor, in the administration building, and everywhere else.

Christian Commitment: Key to Growth

Many declare that church colleges are in trouble and face a dismal future; they are "an endangered species." Inflation and rising costs aggravate problems of inadequate financial resources. Enrollment is declining because of a smaller number of college-bound students, increasing competition for students, a trend away from liberal arts education toward vocational and professional education, the availability of tax-supported colleges with practical programs and low tuition, and governmental regulations which discourage Christian education.

Some church colleges suffer declining enrollments, have increasing costs due to inflation, operate with deficits, and then raise tuition to get more money. Then enrollments decline further, and deficits increase. Many mistakenly have believed that academic education of high quality is incompatible with church-relatedness, and have modified or abandoned the latter. Many also mistakenly have believed that required courses in religion or Christian parietal rules alienate the students and contribute to declining enrollments, and have abandoned these courses and rules. Many have sought to imitate state colleges and have abandoned the emphasis on liberal arts education which frees man from here-and-now, but makes him a citizen of all times and all places, and is calculated to give him a free and soaring spirit. They have offered the same "practical" courses with a value in the marketplace as the secular schools are offering, but have not been able to compete with state-supported secular schools in price charged—tuition.

Those church schools which have striven to remain Christian in all aspects, which have endeavored to remain close to their denomination, which have cultivated every association with the denomination, and indeed tried to strengthen these ties, which have tried to improve and enlarge their service to the denomination, and which have striven ceaselessly to become *more* Christian and not less, have prospered. The denomination has supported them by entrusting them with children and giving them money. Their enrollments have increased, and they have continued to operate in the black and to prosper. These are interesting times. Churches which have unabashedly continued to preach the risen Christ who offers salvation to the world and which have not abandoned this evangelical message have also prospered.

Any careful observer has seen some church colleges either drifting or deliberately moving away from their churches since World War II. Some of them are in trouble. In his foreword to C. Robert Pace's study of *Education and Evangelism: A Profile of Protestant Colleges*, Clark Kerr, chairman of the Carnegie Commission on Higher Education, warned: "Perhaps in greatest difficulty are those mainline denominational colleges that do not now seem committed to either a strong religious philosophy or a strong academic program."

Baylor University's Commitment

It has often been proclaimed that Baylor University was Baptist before there was a Baptist General Convention of Texas and a Southern Baptist Convention, and will be Baptist even if the Convention splits and disintegrates. This is a university that is going to cling to the Baptist churches and serve them. Baylor University is not just an educational institution. It is a Southern Baptist educational institution. It knows its purpose. It knows its identity. It knows who its constituency is. It intends to serve that constituency, and is confident that the churches will back the university and that together they will prosper.

What is the formula for survival and progress for a Southern Baptist college? Have a program of secular education as good as that of any other college. Then have a program of *Christian* education inextricably mixed therewith. This Christian college will be offering more than any secular college. All may not want this product, but many Southern Baptists and others do seek this type of education and will pay for it.

Trustee Responsibility

It is the duty of the trustees elected by the state conventions of Southern Baptists to see that Southern Baptist colleges offer such a program. These are not just personal preferences or prejudices of a Southern Baptist. They are not idealistic dreams either; they are practical, realistic facts. Earl J. McGrath, in his intensive *Study of Southern Baptist Colleges and Universities 1976-77* concludes:

> . . . Those colleges that blow either cold or hot stand the best chance of meeting the hard days ahead. Their lukewarm sister institutions are already experiencing profound academic travails that threaten their survival. The changing times demand that every church-related college continually bring before its deliberative committees—student, faculty, administrative, and trustee—the purposes of the college as they relate to their supporting religious body. The Southern Baptist churches have every right to insist that their colleges offer a

distinctive educational program that produces young men and women dedicated to serving the mission of the church and the needs of the larger society in its local, national, and global settings. The authors of this study believe that the data from the Southern Baptist colleges suggests that their high rating on *esprit* -- highest of any group of comparable institutions in the nation that have taken the IFI (Institutional Functioning Inventory) -- and their sound financial condition are directly related to the clarity of their purpose and mission. . . . It seems reasonable to suppose that their Christian purposes, if advertised broadly, could have drawing power far beyond their denomination, state, or region. One of the major current issues confronting the Southern Baptist churches may well be the degree to which they wish to utilize their colleges and universities as national and international resources for evangelical mission.

Moreover, the January 14, 1980, issue of the *Chronicle of Higher Education* reported that enrollments in church-related colleges across the nation have risen in 1979 by almost two percent -- the greatest increase in any sector of private higher education.

The best practical advice for church-related colleges is the same advice Booz, Allan, and Hamilton would give in recommending a program for the survival and progress of a business, but it has an added Christian dimension: be true to your mission, or perish! This counsel applies to practically all Southern Baptist institutions today. Some of the institutions the government might be willing to take over, and a few could survive as private secular institutions. But the rest will survive only as Southern Baptist institutions.

VII.   New Pathways

The Challenge
of Denominational Relations

Grady C. Cothen

I f one is looking for a unique purpose for existence, an
expanding arena of intellectual confrontation, academic
excitement that goes beyond the ordinary, and a purpose
worthy of the best that is in us all, all this is to be found in the idea of a
Christian college.

A Hazardous Undertaking

The presence of a Christian denomination in the world of higher
education frequently causes discomfort for its constituents and for the
educational community at large. Each is zealous for its purposes and
integrity. Each has its own value system and is concerned about its
preservation. Frequently, each looks askance at the other as though these
purposes and values are mutually exclusive.

Another confrontation inevitably arises from relationships between
the sponsoring body and the sponsored institution. The expectations of
both are at once apt to be too high and too low. There is sometimes lack of
understanding in higher education of the nature and function of the
denomination. Equally the sponsors frequently fail to understand the
nature and function of an institution of higher learning. Many institutions
which looked to the sponsor for support—financial, moral, student—have

found that the tie to the school seems to be for control and not support purposes. Each has looked for response to the other in ways poorly understood or unexpected.

The Classic Problem

These problems are intensified by the nature of the educational experience.

There are those who believe that the terms "Christian" and "college" are mutually exclusive. They believe that if an institution is explicitly Christian, then it cannot be a college. A college searches for knowledge and truth, but a Christian claims that revelation contains ultimate truth. The commitment of the college is to the search for truth, requiring freedom. The commitment of a Christian is to revealed truth, and if this becomes a rigid commitment, it may tend toward dogmatism. Thus, some believe that a college cannot be committed to being Christian.

This does seem to be an inherent problem. The business of the college is knowledge, ideas. It is involved in the acquisition, transmission, examination, and preservation of knowledge and/or truth. The college lives with empirical evidence. It examines philosophical, scientific, economic, sociological, and psychological theory. The college lives in the land of the eternally tentative. Its value systems relate to empirical evidence, to integrity of methodology, and to the occasional intuitive flash known to all scientists.

On the other hand, the Christian institution is also concerned with revelation, the unveiling by God of himself in the person of Jesus Christ and the sacred scripture. The Christian deals with absolutes, with those matters that are assumed by faith to be truth, and thus are not usually subject to examination by the same tools that are typically used by the educational institution. One formulation of the difficulty may be faith *vis-a-vis* the so-called scientific method.

Values in the Christian institution are of extreme importance. These values have to do with the worthwhileness of every person, integrity, honesty, scriptural truth, the family, and the person and purposes of God. While the secular college is concerned with temporal things, the Christian institution is concerned also with eternal values. Any college is interested in the transmission of general knowledge and values; the Christian institution is interested also in the transmission of particular values, for the Christian believes that he has found ultimate truth and worth. The transmission of these concepts is crucial to the purpose of the Christian college. It was for value-propagation as well as education that the organizers of the denomination and Christians in general founded institutions of higher education. Many educators and Christians in the curious milieu of the modern world consider these apparent conflicts to be inevitable and inescapable, and reconciliation of these points of view to be impossible.

The Dilemma: Apparent or Real?

It is my own opinion, however, that the conflict is more apparent than real, and that the issues are not so clean-cut and simplistic as they seem to be. For example, look for a moment at the ingredients in this apparent dilemma. The educational institution, by its very nature, assumes the burden thrust upon it by society. Its obligation is to know what has been discovered or what is in process. It must deal with whatever ideas scholars choose to discuss. The institution of higher learning cannot afford to opt out of the discussion, however unpleasant, uncertain or unthinkable it may be. The business of the college is ideas, knowledge, intellectual confrontation, and investigation. In modern times this assignment cannot be excluded by the founders, nor its pursuit inhibited by preconceptions. When the ideas of modern science, philosophy, sociology, and the interpretations of history seem to challenge the tenets of Christian faith, the conflict must be joined, and the educational institution has neither the power nor prerogative to decline to participate.

If the concepts of Christianity and those of higher learning seem to be mutually exclusive, it is in the Christian college that they can be integrated. Indeed, it is in this particular that the Christian college has its greatest opportunity and holds forth to troubled man his greatest hope.

Whatever else may be said about the institution of higher education that claims the name Christian, it must maintain a level of educational excellence that is unchallenged in its educational community. For the Christian college to be less than intellectually proficient in our times would be to be less than Christian. For the Christian institution to require less of its students in the general disciplines of education than the secular institutions require would be unthinkable and would violate basic Christian commitment to values. Let me reiterate—the arena of intellectual confrontation cannot be circumscribed by the Christian's convictions related to revelation. This is not to say that he compromises his conviction about revelation; it is to say that the intellectual arena is defined by the secular community, and while the Christian institution must deal with its own peculiar interests, it cannot opt out of the confrontations of the intellectual community and remain an accredited or a credible institution.

Curiously, however, the place where the institution of higher learning called "Christian" fails most often is not in the academic arena. Most often its greatest lack is in what we call, for lack of better phraseology, "the Christian dimension." Baptists have traditionally been dissenters: freedom of conscience and freedom of investigation are basically Baptist principles. Of course, there are those few Baptists who would make authoritarians of us all. However, there is nothing in true Baptist philosophy, polity, governance, or theology that inhibits investigation. God and scripture, in my judgment, are not threatened by science. Indeed, science seems to disturb science far more often than it does religion. An interesting illustration of this fact came recently out of Mountainview, California, in the reports of the Pioneer probes of Venus. The Pioneer project manager, Charles Hall, said at the Ames Research Center that the satellite has discovered far more primordial argon and neon in the Venus atmosphere than was expected. These findings challenge most theories of the formation of the solar system, and Hall said, "We are still baffled at this time by the meaning of the measurements."

For those who have made absolutes of the findings of science and have criticized the absolutes of Christian faith, it is interesting to note that the conclusions of anthropologists related to the beginning of the race have similarly been disrupted by recent discoveries of their science. This is in no sense a criticism of anthropology, astronomy, physics, or any of the other sciences. It is to say that the science of today may turn out to be inadequate tomorrow. The absolutes of the scientists are always on shaky ground, since the conclusions of science are constantly being revised on the basis of new evidence. Religion does not live primarily in the land of empirical evidence.

The Unique Purpose

The Christian institution of higher education should never lose sight of the fact that its unique purpose for existence is not to be found in its educational dimension alone. This does not denigrate the educational function; but if the Christian college is to fulfill its purpose, there must be a clear and unswerving commitment to the idea of the Christian dimension. The Christian ideal must be firmly entrenched in the official documents, in the statement of purpose, in the philosophical positions espoused, in the mind of its board of trustees; and the Christian dimension must receive the constant attention of the administration, faculty, students and constituency.

The Student and the Denominational Perspective

Some years ago, Kenneth Scott Latourette said that the first part of an institution of Christian higher education to become secularized is the student body, followed quickly by the faculty. Let us look for a minute at the element of the student in the Christian community of learning.

When students come to college, they have been the center of the home, of the family. Many times they have been the center of attention of the church. Quite often they have been "wheels" at school, big men and women on campus. Immediately in the alien environment they are thrust into a living situation with hundreds of other young people who are similar but also vastly different. They are thrown into a classroom situation with probably the heaviest academic load they have ever known. They feel alone and isolated. They are for the first time on their own, facing crucial life decisions. Most of them are going to decide within the next few years whom they will marry and when. They will make up their minds about their careers. They will decide about their life-style and whether it will fit in the kind of world they want to live in. Values of parents must become the student's values, or he must find his own; otherwise he will have no values at all.

These students are free for the first time, in the main, from parental support, guidance, and the warmth of the family situation. It is inevitable that some of them are going to overreact. Some will be frightened and isoloated in the midst of difficulty and what they conceive to be a hostile environment (and faculty people have been known to become hostile on occasion!). Some of them will have such a good time, since they are free from parental supervision for the first time, that they will overreact. They are confronting the world without the accustomed limitations and family shielding. Now they have to make it on their own. They must face individuals as individuals, and the peer influence is very strong. Some studies show that after the age of twelve the strongest influence on the life of the young person is not the school, the church, or the family, but that of his peers. During these crucial years the student must grow up, and all of this must be accomplished in a relatively brief period of time.

The sponsoring denomination needs to understand and be patient with the problems the Christian college is helping the students to solve.

Understanding the Faculty

The second element in the Christian college for the denomination to understand is the faculty. One of my best academicians said to me several years ago, "Faculty are strange people." Of necessity they must be a little unusual, or they could not tolerate teaching "bonehead English" to freshmen year after year, repeating the same history course endlessly, and dealing with the same basic elementary studies in chemistry and a dozen other disciplines again and again. Faculty people live with ideas and argumentation. It is a way of life. Some people play checkers or chess. Faculty people also play with ideas. It is the way they live, and it is a part of the nature of the intellectual life. Occasionally they will argue vociferously an idea that they do not believe at all, simply to test the idea or the intellect of the opponent. It is mandatory that faculty deal with ideas.

The ideas they deal with do not have to be tested in the supermarket or the business world. Many of their concepts may seem foreign to those who do not live in academe, and indeed they are, but twenty years from now they may become a part of the common fabric of society. The faculty must deal with the latest discovery in subject matter, and must examine it assiduously. Whatever a scholar does in sociology must be investigated by sociologists, even if it is obviously limited. Whatever a scholar says about chemistry must be investigated by the chemists. As a result, faculty seem to be dealing often with intellectual fads, but if the scholar does not examine these matters and evaluate them, he may be left behind in his own discipline.

COTHEN: DENOMINATIONAL RELATIONS   77

Faculty people in a Baptist college are Christian people. They frequently, however, describe their faith not in the terms of the accepted jargon of theology, but in terms of the disciplines which they teach. The scientist, as he begins to talk about Christian faith and creation, may become involved in quantum mechanics. It is inevitable that the scientist will talk about reality in terms of the modern physical principles which he knows, or thinks he knows. The psychologist will talk in terms of behaviorism and determinism or whatever the latest terminology may be. This is not bad, but is necessary in the constant search for honesty and consistency.

It is inevitable that many concepts which the Christian accepts because they are a part of revelation must raise questions in the minds of faculty people because they are not only Christians who believe in revelation but they are also scientists or historians who believe in empirical evidence; and revelation and empirical evidence may seem to be poles apart. So faculty people are endlessly asking questions, and they are always wondering how a particular aspect of Christian faith affects what they understand in their discipline as they pursue knowledge.

Further, these Christians who participate in academic disciplines are apt to be more interested in the way people live than in what they say they believe. We might even say that they are often more interested in the nature of the Christian life than in academic Christian theology. This is not to say that they are not interested in orthodoxy; it is to say that they are apt to describe it in terms of their everyday life; and so far as I am able to ascertain, this is thoroughly Christian.

What Is a Christian Dimension?

Since I have asserted that the Christian college is more likely to lose the Christian dimension than the educational dimension, let me turn our attention to the nature of the Christian dimension. Church people often expect the Christian college to be a duplication of the church, with an instructional program including a large chunk of extended Sunday School. They would also like frequent worship in a church-like atmosphere. Many seem to want the students to be protected from ideas that challenge faith.

In fact, the true Christian dimension in a college may differ sharply, and may be far more difficult to achieve. One element of this Christian dimension is surely an atmosphere which is conducive to faith. The discussion of the ultimate nature of Christian and spiritual values must be offered in an atmosphere which makes possible serious consideration. This atmosphere was once described by Dr. William Mitchell, dean of the College of Liberal Arts of Oklahoma Baptist University, as follows:

> The Christian dimension is an atmosphere which reflects the virtues of Christian tenets: namely, love and respect for one's fellowman, responsibility in words and actions, zeal in search for truth and knowledge, integrity, humility, reverence for and faith in God, and belief that each person has purpose in his life's actions.

Demonstration of the Christian qualities in life is crucially important to the Christian dimension in the educational institution. Among other things, this will mean a restraint on conduct that outrages conscience, and a general observance of Christian moral and ethical standards—not by reason of coercion but by reason of personal commitment to these values and standards. The Christian dimension certainly implies that a vital element is the quality of persons who are present in the community. It is essential for the Christian dimension that the principal actors on this stage be committed Christian people who try to live the life, who are committed to Christian values, who are interested in the goals of the institution, and who will be sensitive to the interests and needs of the young people. Without such a demonstration of Christian living, it is unlikely that students will become seriously interested in Christianity.

A significant element of the Christian dimension is a fair and honest treatment of the Christian faith. This means a recognition of the validity of the Christian religion as a discipline; just and honest presentation in the classroom of the tenets of the faith; and responsible treatment of the Christian religion in chapel, in focus-week observances, and wherever faith is discussed. It means that there will be no intellectual slight or minimizing of the faith if faith is to be a true dimension of the institution itself. It means, of course, devotion to God and to the church. Of particular significance to young people in this kind of society is devotion to Christian attitudes toward people, realistically putting into effect the process of Christian caring in human relationships of the community.

The tools of the community of Christians are those of reason. This community must be maintained by reason as much as this is possible. There must not be any coercion in matters of religion. There cannot be coercion in matters of intellect. Coercion will be the tool of the academic Christian community only as it is necessary to maintain the integrity and health of the community. The uses of power must be limited to those essential to the creation and maintenance of valid academic and Christian life. In short, this community cannot exist as long as disruption of the academic process or personal rights of any member of the community is allowed. Of necessity, there must be some limitations on overtly unchristian conduct of members of the community. In part these limitations must be accepted voluntarily. In part they must be enforced to prevent the supporting society from turning on this unique community. This will mean that Christian ethical and moral standards will be presented and defended, and that there must be in the community a constant and consistent application of Christian principles in human relationships.

If the Christian higher educational institution is to survive in this kind of world, these tasks must be attempted, and these fundamental precepts must be involved. The Christian educational community is a place of commitment to each person and commitment to the institution. The community of interest between the faculty and students must be real. Thus the faculty must be concerned about the total general welfare of the student. This inevitably involves the sense of Christian ministry to the student: in his problems of maturation, choice of a profession, selection of a lifemate, religious crisis, adoption of a life-style—in short, his setting of the course of his life.

The Christian commitment in an intellectual community means helping students in the intellectual struggle caused by the pluralism in the educational world and society in which we live. It will require helping them to understand religion as a discipline and as a relationship of their personal life.

The Intellectual Confrontation

To summarize, Christian educators must constantly bear in mind that one of the principal functions of an institution of higher learning called Christian in our time is an honest confrontation of the intellectual problems of the disciplines. Many of the conclusions of the social sciences and other disciplines in our time seem to be diametrically opposed to the conclusions of the Christian faith. The influence of secularism, humanism, and naturalism in our time is often antithetical to the basic understandings of the Christian faith. This battle has been joined, to the great suffering of the Christian religion in many institutions where faith is not given fair consideration. Most students come out of this pluralistic society where the assumptions of secularism, humanism, and naturalism are accepted as the conclusions of learning. This makes the task of the Christian institution much more difficult, but it is perhaps at this very point where the greatest victories are to be won by faith. If the Christian institution does not enter this arena, it is inevitable that the problems will be so great and the losses so significant that the Christian institution may not be able to survive as a viable entity in a pluralistic society.

Interestingly, it is the very nature of this conflict that makes the idea of a Christian college so important to our time. It is a dangerous idea. The very existence of such institutions is threatened by the secularism that denies the need for them. Often the humaneness of the liberal arts is treated as an adequate substitute for a true Christian dimension. A substantial number of institutions themselves have abandoned the basic purposes which called them into existence. Academicians sometimes lead them to turn away from their true goals. Students attempt to secularize Christian institutions. The institutions themselves sometimes do not face fairly the intellectual confrontations that are mandatory. The constituents frequently do not understand the nature of the educational experience and are frightened by the intellectual confrontations.

All of these difficulties call not for a lessening of influence or abandoning of purpose. They demand a new measure of dedication and rededication by the institutions themselves, and by the people who make up their publics, to a new emphasis upon their nature and purpose.

If Christians had not been involved in the processes of education across the centuries, it would be necessary now to bring into existence Christian higher education. The moral and ethical climate in the society, the enforced secularity of state-supported higher education, and the condition of man make mandatory the idea of Christian higher learning. The state of the nation, the hurting world, confused men, and the disintegrating society all cry out for confrontation between the inteliect and the spirit.

Those with the convictions of faith and the courage of those convictions are strategically located at an intellectual crossroads of dangerous opportunity. The denomination and the university are twice blessed—with faith and learning.

VIII. New Pathways

Developing a Viable Campus Ministry

L. D. Johnson

My introduction to college chaplaincy began somewhat inauspiciously. Two days after moving my books in I was invited to a meeting of the Wesley Foundation on campus, and went thinking how nice to get acquainted with some of the religiously-minded students. I sat down beside a girl who introduced herself as "Fran." She fixed me with an appraising eye and said, "So you are Furman's first full-time chaplain." I acknowledged that I was, and she announced evenly, "Well, I mean no disrespect, but I don't think you can do the job." "Oh," I stammered, trying not to appear as disconcerted as I felt, "why not?" "Because you are a Baptist preacher, and you are too old." She had me dead to rights on all three counts. I am a Baptist, a preacher, and I was then (13 years ago) already two decades beyond the magical age of 30. Here I am, still unconvinced that I can't do this job.

My years as chaplain and professor of religion have been the most satisfying of my vocational life. The description of chaplain as a person with preaching and pastoral skills and academic qualifications was designed by Vice-President and Provost F. W. Bonner, under whom I work and who gives important administrative support to this concept of campus ministry. I have faculty status and teach two courses per year. Here both parts of my vocational world came together—ministering both as pastor and professor, a combination that seems right for me and my colleague in chaplaincy, Dr. James M. Pitts, who is also now in his thirteenth year in our office.

Dual Role — Pastor and Professor

Religion as an academic discipline often has had a bad press in college circles, even in the church-related college. Sometimes it is seen as a glorified Sunday School exercise, the professor of religion caricatured as the unsuccessful parish minister who couldn't make it in the demanding atmosphere of the local church, so retreated with his homilies and moralisms to the religion department of his denomination's church college. Inasmuch as there was occasionally more fact than fiction in that description, others sought to correct the low esteem in which religion was held as an academic pursuit. Jealous for their department's academic reputation, some professors of religion practiced a strict separation of classroom and confession. They made it plain that the teaching of religion was a distinctly different task from the practice thereof. To establish the desired distance between themselves and the church they became observers or even detractors. They saw no more connection between what they were teaching and the life of faith on campus than if they were teaching courses in mathematics.

For example, in 1967, the year I became a college chaplain, the Commission on Higher Education of the National Council of Churches convened a conference of the leaders of departments of religious studies in the United States. They gave almost no attention in the discussions and papers to the extracurricular aspects of religious studies. This is not to suggest that professors of religion are indifferent to the life of Christian faith. It is to suggest that they often do not see themselves as particularly involved in or responsible for campus ministry, or campus ministers as partners in the teaching of religion in the college. In that same year, 1967, the National Association of Campus Ministries also met, and though they organized discussion groups and panels on a variety of concerns, they gave no attention to the development of research and teaching in departments of religious studies.

What we have sought to do at Furman is consciously to relate academic and confessional aspects of Christian faith. Some will argue that this is not possible, but we remain unconvinced. When we began in 1967 to frame a vision of campus ministry, my colleague and I came early to the decision that we are first of all ministers, not directors of religious activities. We would function as ministers in residence on campus, not organizers of sacred volley ball games. We wanted to be known as clergymen, for that is who we are. Would not the image of "minister" get in the way of ministry to certain students? Yes, it would and it has. I think I never overcame the totally unscientific and wholly irrational judgment of Fran about me. More than a few times we have been victimized by stereotypical thinking.

Potential Liabilities in Pastoral Role

Once I found myself being berated repeatedly in the college newspaper by a student of whom I knew little except his name and record of high academic achievement. He seemed intent on destroying any influence I might have on campus, making frequent comments about the chaplain's "presumed intelligence." Two years after his graduation this young man drove several hundred miles to visit me in order to apologize and explain why he had had such angry feelings. While I was still a pastor I had conducted a graveside service for this young man's father, whom I did not know, as he was not a member of my congregation. The son was bitter at God for letting his father die so suddenly, and as he heard me speaking for God the words of comfort he unconciously transferred his anger toward God upon me, the visible witness to God's Presence. Neither he nor I understood what was going on until years after it had happened.

Sometimes the transference is not so hard to perceive. Until the student learns differently, he may identify us with his image of the moralizing, judgmental, self-righteous, ineffectual "preacher" of the movies, or maybe even of his own experience. Once two young men came to talk about a friend who was neck-deep in pot and despair. "That was the hardest thing I've done since I have been at this place," said one as they shuffled in and sat down. "What is that?" I asked. "Walking in that door." "Tell me about it," I said. "Well," he said, "I walk by outside and look in the window at all those people sitting there in the office and say to myself, 'There they are, all of them waiting to go in and get their weekly 30-minute religious fix.'" I do not pretend that there are no liabilities to being who I am, a pastoral minister on campus.

But that is who I am. I am a minister of God with a graduate degree designed to help me understand people's psyches and what goes wrong with them. So is my associate. We are not pseudo-psychiatrists, nor do we aspire to be. Our psychiatric colleagues have their language of salvation and we have ours. We would argue that ours not only is appropriate for us to use in helping distressed students, but that it is more needed than theirs in many cases. Those who do need psychiatric evaluation and/or therapy are quickly put in good care. However, we are increasingly confident that the basic crises of most college students in this generation are indeed spiritual in nature. The questions of meaning, of ultimacy, of God, underlie most of the "problems" I listen to day after day.

Occasionally our identity as ministers erects another kind of barrier. The student who sees the minister as a bulwark against the invasion of the student's mind by any evidence or idea that would require him to enlarge his religious vision is disappointed in us. To him we belong to the enemy camp. We are not stroking and reassuring him in his resistance to intellectual and spiritual growth. Instead, we are part of the challenge which he may see as a threat to the categories in which he has grown comfortable. Indeed, we are especially disappointing to him because he expected better things of us. We try to coax him out of his ignorance rather than to comfort him in it. So we may not be given a chance by such a student until somebody cracks him open and he can no longer cling to the small island which he thought was the totality of being. Then he will come to us ready to accept help in discovering a larger island. We may even be able to help him understand that the largest island he will ever stand upon is only a tiny dot on the horizon of being.

Significance of Academic Identity

Thus our vision of campus ministry is first of all that of pastoral ministers. The other side is that we also see ourselves as teachers. Both full-time chaplains have faculty status and teach courses in the religion department. We do not wish to be thought of, either by students or faculty, as the Baptist preachers on campus who perform sacerdotal functions (such as they are) and provide denominational sanction. This is not to suggest that we or colleagues have no responsibilities toward the Convention, but that we are first of all pastoral and teaching ministers in the college.

Does being a professor get in the way of being a chaplain? Yes, sometimes it does. The chaplain-professor perhaps has to work a bit harder than do some of his colleagues at being taken seriously as a teacher.

Wearing both hats is cumbersome, especially when the student you are counselling is also the student you are teaching. Unless you have your own role identity clear, you may have difficulty clarifying it to students and colleagues. Needless to say, I believe that this is possible. I favor this model of campus ministry not only because it meets my personal vocational needs but also because I believe that it maximizes the potential for meaningful campus ministry.

Two years after we adopted the model of pastor-teacher for chaplaincy at Furman, the impressive work of the late Kenneth Underwood and his colleagues was published. This was the Danforth Study of Campus Ministries, the findings published shortly after Underwood's death, and appearing in 1969 under the title, *The Church, The University, and Social Policy*. Jim Pitts and I found the Danforth Study exciting, reassuring, and instructive. It confirmed our belief that we were on the right track in shaping a viable model for campus ministry.

In a summary report, called "New Wine," the Commission on the Danforth Study of Campus Ministries described their task as one of seeking to define and understand the "crisis in the campus ministry . . . caused in part by the fact that it as a profession inherits the problems of both institutions. Campus ministers are uncertain of their relations to other members of the church and the university, and of the nature of ministry within the university. They frequently feel isolated from students, faculty and administration, as well as from parish ministers and the governing powers of the church. They do not know whether to seek academic credentials giving them equality of status with faculty or to act on the basis of the traditional patterns of ministry. They seek legitimate modes of response to student demands for new approaches to education and society, while yet desiring to relate themselves responsibly to the traditions of governance and authority within both the church and the university."[1]

Pastor, Priest, Prophet, King

Six years of study brought the Commission to the conclusion that the "new wine" of campus ministry lies in the biblical and historic roles of

[1] "New Wine," in *A Report of the Commission on the Danforth Study of Campus Ministries* (St. Louis: Danforth Foundation, 1969), p. 4.

minister as pastor, priest, prophet, and king. These roles are foreshadowed in the Old Testament and fully embodied in Jesus Christ, and are historically normative for the Christian community. The campus minister who models his vocation in those four modes will have a clear notion of who he is and how he relates to the several constituencies for which he has spiritual responsibility—students, faculty, administration, and staff.

Administrative Functions

With a view to the limitations of space I shall briefly describe our understanding of the meaning of the four modes of campus ministry. Let me reverse the order suggested by the Danforth Commission, betraying my preferences. Least enjoyable, but nevertheless necessary, is governance. Chaplains have administrative duties. They coordinate religious activities under the umbrella of a Religious Council composed of the chief officer of each of the fifteen or so chartered religious organizations on campus. Charters are granted by Student Government and are required for participation in the life of the university. It is occasionally the unpleasant task of the chaplains to decline requests by outside religious groups to come on campus to recruit. A college campus is a happy hunting ground for every conceivable cult. We have had skirmishes with almost every variety. The authority of the chaplains includes the responsibility to prevent Furman's campus from being a game preserve for religious trophy seekers. Eight volunteer chaplains, all ordained clergy persons who represent on-going religious groups on campus, assist us in the work of campus ministry.They are chosen by their own church and approved by the chaplains, and give approximately one-half day each per week to this ministry.

As a further aspect of governance responsibility, we organize and administer a Religion in Life Convocation series of fourteen lectures annually. With the assistance of a student-faculty committee, such lectures/programs are planned to examine the religious and moral dimensions of pressing human and national concerns. The RIL convocations are a part of a larger university-wide Cultural Life Program in which all students are required to participate, being given wide latitude in their choices of events to attend. These may include concerts, recitals, plays, selected movies, lectures of special interest, as well as the RIL series.

The chaplains also have responsibility for an annual Furman Pastors' School, four days of intensive continuing theological and pastoral education for clergy persons of all denominations. Both the lecturers and the attendants represent a wide variety of denominational and geographical place. The chaplain sits on the Administrative Council of the University, and the associate chaplain is responsible for the administration of an in-service training program for all church-related vocations students.

Prophetic Role Acknowledged

Secondly, we acknowledge a prophetic role in campus ministry. We wish we were courageous enough and had faith enough to be truly prophetic. The prophets were gadflies. They were continually challenging the status quo and the powers that kept it and profited by it. Ministers in local congregations do not find the prophet mantle an easy and comfortable one. No less so does the college chaplain who believes that he is called to be more than a nice, well-meaning, but essentially powerless and harmless friend of homesick and lovesick students. Few of us have the flair or the ability of a Bill Coffin, but the call to be prophet causes us to wrestle with the moral implications of policy-makers' decisions and to call upon them to wrestle with those issues. Where there is no prophetic voice in the college, as in society, pragmatism goes unchecked. We would not presume to suggest that there are no prophetic words spoken save those uttered on occasion by the college chaplain, but we would contend that the chaplain who can assume no prophetic role in the life of the university is essentially a powerless religious eunuch. If anyone in the college community may be expected to raise the issue of values and priorities, or of the nature of persons and the Christian understanding of life and interpersonal relationships, who better to do it than the chaplain?

Priest on Campus

Campus ministry has a third dimension, the proclamation and demonstration of the historic Christian faith through worship and ministry. In this biblical sense, the chaplain is also priest of God to God's people. We do not confuse campus and church. We are not called to minister to and administer the affairs of an ongoing community of faith which meets regularly to acknowledge and celebrate the lordship of Christ and its oneness in Him. Still there is an element of the priestly in campus ministry. I see myself as more than your wise (sometimes), friendly, father-figure. I am a minister of Christ, dispenser of his grace, and therefore a priest. Inasmuch as I take seriously the New Testament teaching about priesthood of believers, I do not suppose that I have some special dispensation reserved for clergy. But I do have a special and strategic opportunity to be priest to my brothers and sisters at Furman.

That opportunity is expressed in the setting of a Sunday worship service on campus in which one of the chaplains preaches the sermon in a student-planned and student-oriented service of worship. It is actualized in marriage counselling, and the occasional wedding where two students or former students request the chaplains to be the officiating ministers. It is expressed in hospital ministry to persons from the Furman community who have a hospital experience. We seek to be priests to the bereaved to help them experience God's grace and strength as they do their grieving. And we function daily as priests to young people wrestling with the painful issues of faith and doubt. Nowhere do I sense the Presence more or become more keenly aware of the sacred than in those moments when I know that God and some fellow human being have accorded me the honor of being priest on a specific occasion in a special set of circumstances.

Shepherd of the Fold

At no point do the modes of ministry converge and merge into one another so clearly as in the areas of priesting and shepherding. The priest is also the pastor. If priesting looks at ministry from the perspective of bringing God's grace to persons who need it, shepherding looks at ministry from the perspective of bringing persons who need it to God's grace. Pastoral care puts persons above programs and activities. It is aimed at providing aid and guidance to the individual in his search for integrity and meaning in his life, especially in times of great stress or pain or despair.

In the performance of the ministry of pastoral care we find traditional moralistic approaches of ministers generally ineffective. "The Bible says" approach to counselling only alienates students. This is not because what the Bible says is either unimportant or irrelevant to students. It is rather that most seek to understand *why* what the Bible says is applicable to their condition and *how* they may appropriate its promise of deliverance. Using the Bible as a club in moralistic, judgmental pronouncement is counterproductive in pastoral care everywhere, most especially in the chaplain's office.

Pastoral caring is more than a "There, there, you poor dear" pat on the shoulder. We offer more than tea and sympathy, although we dispense a good deal of both around our place. The skills gained in training and experience enable us to assist persons to sort out the factors of their experience interrupting the free flow and fulfillment of their lives, examine what options are available, and then make a plan to implement that option which is apt to bring them the largest measure of spiritual and mental wholeness.

To do this kind of ministry requires a large amount of time and patience. Involved as well is a great amount of "presence and availability." A student may walk in with a casual air and without an appointment, sit down and begin to unload a staggering burden of pain, grief, guilt, or despair. The ministry of presence and availability is nowhere more crucial than in college chaplaincy. Sometimes we help without knowing that we have done so. Not infrequently an alumnus writes back to thank us "for what you meant to me." We recall no specific "ministry" to that person. But we were present, and we represented something that at some critical time was a redeeming factor in that person's life. Needless to say, the disappointments and rewards accruing to the pastoral counselor are the sources of his keenest feelings about his vocation.

The presenting event that brings the student to the chaplain may be any of a multiplicity of distressing and disturbing interruptions of the even flow of his life. Some of the most common are disruption of the family life through divorce of the parents or the death of a family member. Others include stress between parent and student, or stress between student and girl/boy friend, roommate or other valued person. Not infrequently the agenda is sexual—an unwanted pregnancy, guilt over the sexualizing of a relationship, despair about being trapped in a relationship, fear of being a homosexual, or declaration of being homosexual with the quest for guidance. Most frequently the nature of the presenting problem is basically religious and spiritual. "I can no longer believe as I was brought up to believe. What is happening to my faith? Why do you believe in God? What do I have to believe to be a Christian? How can I reconcile what I now know of the universe with the Bible?" To respond to such occasions as the above requires more than a facile tongue and a pocketful of ready-made answers.

Theological Commitment Undergirds Daily Schedule

I have described new pathways to developing a viable campus ministry by outlining the job description of the chaplains at Furman University. That may reflect an enormous egotism, but at least it has the merit of reflecting a specific vision of what chaplaincy ought to be. And vision in campus ministry is evidently in short supply. In the spring, 1979, issue of *The NICM Journal* a Lilly Endowment study of theological values on which campus ministers base their work was reported. The study was in connection with a highly competitive "Grants Programs in Higher Education" offer made by the Lilly Endowment. Of 280 proposals made by campus ministers requesting grants, 41 per cent lacked any statement concerning their vision of ministry, although specifically requested by the grantor to supply such a statement. And of the applicants who did comply with the requirement, more than half stated their vision by describing their program rather than by spelling out the theological assumptions underlying the program. Only 10 per cent of the visions of all 280 proposals examined were theological in character. The reporter of the study in the Journal suggests a disturbing conclusion: "Campus ministers do painfully little theological reflection."[2]

We believe that our vision of college chaplaincy has been formed out of our theological understanding of the meaning of ministry. We also believe that it reflects understanding of the nature of the college student and of the late 20th-century college scene in the United States. We commend the model of chaplain-teacher in the biblical modes of minister as shepherd, priest, prophet, and king. We believe it to be particularly appropriate for the church-related college.

---

[2]George Wiley, "Toward Parish and Community, Unreflectively," *The NICM Journal,* XXIV (Spring, 1979), 15.

IX. New Pathways

Developing a Value-Centered Curriculum

E. Eugene Hall

John Milton wrote "Of Education" at the end of an era. Shaped alike by Renaissance and Reformation spirit, Milton turned in 1644 to the task of describing the ends of education and how they could be attained, principally through a study of the classical languages and the wisdom set down in the ancient writings. But the age of the Puritan Revolution in England had brought to consciousness the reality of sweeping change in education—particularly a thrust toward the future for the discovery of wisdom emerging from the reassessment of the past and an examination of the present development of man's expanding experience in knowing.

While Milton's recommendations were timed unfortunately for adoption, his insights are interesting to educators today who seek to accommodate a values orientation to curriculum change. Milton observes that "the end of learning is to repair the ruins of our first parents by regaining to know God aright and out of that knowledge to love Him, to imitate Him, to be like Him. . . by possessing our souls of true virtue, which being united to the heavenly grace of faith, makes up the highest perfection."[1] He recommends the study of languages to facilitate the

---

[1] John Milton, *Areopagitica and of Education*, ed. George H. Sabine (New York: Appleton-Century-Crofts, 1951), p. 59.

assimilation of the wisdom variously set down in the past. Therein, he believes, one may gain appreciation for justice and equity, virtue and true labor, manly and liberal exercise, incredible diligence and courage, in order to become perfect in the knowledge of personal duty and steadfast as pillars of the state.

Milton endorsed cultivation of ". . .that act of reason which in ethics is called *proairesis* [deliberate choice] that . . .[students] may with some judgment contemplate upon moral good and evil. Then will be required a special reinforcement of constant and sound indoctrinating to set them right and firm, instructing them more amply in the knowledge of virtue and the hatred of vice . . . ."[2]

The course recommended would fit "a man to perform justly, skillfully, and magnanimously, all the offices both private and public, of peace and war."[3]

Milton's Ideals Applied to the Modern Church-Related College

Were one to cast Milton's scheme in contemporary language it would not be out of place as the introduction to a course of study in a church-related liberal arts college in the last decades of the twentieth century. Our analysis of that catalog would lead us to describe the curriculum as heritage-based and values-oriented, with strong emphases upon classical knowledge and languages. The values noted in Milton's tractate include Christian virtues, faith, justice, equity, diligence, patriotism, manliness, freedom, courage, duty, good moral choices, and aesthetic expression—all worthy of cultivation in our age as well as his.

In the decades since the Second World War, however, we have self-consciously and diligently avoided attention to such purposes in our educational programs. This tendency may be explained in terms of a natural disappointment in systems which failed to educate for peaceful life, which did not foster the resolution of conflict except through widespread destruction of life and property, and which affirmed once again the nature of man's inhumanity. With a spirit of failure educational institutions picked up their tasks in unsettled times characterized by disruptive

---

[2]Milton, p. 66.

[3]*Ibid.*, p. 62.

conflicts, a continuation of the draft, a growing secular spirit, and a rootless and uncertain tenor in American life. The success of our principal global rival in technologies leading to the first breakthrough in space caused the assignment of a national educational priority to science. A corollary de-emphasis on humanistic studies contributed to the espousal of value-free, less subjective approaches to education, particularly in the rapidly expanding publicly-supported colleges and universities.

Traditionally less subject to external assignment of educational priorities and less involved in study and research in technological fields, church-related liberal arts colleges and universities retained a humanistic general education core described, probably most often, as heritage-based. The framework for the curriculum was essentially historical, whether one examined the two-semester course sequence in Western civilization or its counterpart in British and/or American literature. Chronology governed instruction and provided its pattern. To some extent the study of the biblical record accommodated this understanding as it was regarded either as "history" or "literature," generally treated developmentally.

A breakthrough, occasioned perhaps by an American occupation of Japan, a conflict in Korea, an essential consideration of a major non-western power (the Soviet Union), and the necessity of closely observing tensions in the Middle East, and rapid change in Africa and the two Chinas opened the Western heritage-based curricula to a consideration of non-Western culture. Comparisons spawned questions regarding relative merit. Good could be seen from varied vantage points in the success of institutions. Contrasting failures gave rise to questions, the resolution of which required a consideration of values.

Early Emphasis on Clarifying Values

In the early years of the past decade in elementary and secondary schools the *clarification of values* was introduced. Mirror to the secular society, these exercises or approaches sought to awaken within the student awareness of societal and individual values operative in his personal or institutional experience. The student was typically presented with a series of decisions relating, for example, to problems in family living. When his evaluation of the hypothetical situation was concluded, he was led to review the reasons for his decisions, to discover (clarify) the values operative in the process. This approach is valuable in areas of student experience such as family and home relationships, friendships, career decisions, attitudes toward public and political institutions, civic responsibilities, religious commitment and the like.[4]

Reliance on Reaffirming and Inculcating Values

Perhaps a second approach to the consideration of values within the curriculum could have been found at any time in their history as a part of the educational programs of church-related liberal arts colleges. While there is probably no institution of higher education which would use Milton's term referred to above, "sound *indoctrinating* to set... [students] right and firm, instructing them more amply in the knowledge of virtue and the hatred of vice," there are more acceptable descriptive terms which might be used: *inculcation or reaffirmation of values.*

A Christian college is by definition concerned with values which emanate from goals implied, if not explicitly stated, which shape the academic programs of the institution. Traditionally, for example, such colleges have afforded corporate experiences of worship in required chapel services. Frequently institutions alternated general programming with religious services to afford the student body emphases which were values-oriented, experiences chosen to foster the acquisition of information through public addresses or to heighten aesthetic appreciation through dramatic or musical performances. In the fifties, typically a school would require students to attend three "chapels" each week. Relaxation of the requirement to twice weekly, then once weekly followed in many institutions, but the emphasis upon moral and spiritual values in the chapel programs continued.

Christian colleges sought, as well, to inculcate values through their residential programs. Conduct of students both on and off campus was regulated. The student handbook contained a listing of prohibitions designed to cultivate adherence to values in relationships necessitated, it was felt, by the freedom experienced by students away from parental supervision probably for the first time. The *in loco parentis* philosophy of student development tended to continue emphases of the homes from

[4]A discussion of this approach may be found in Louis E. Roshe, Merrill Harmon and Sidney B. Simon, *Values and Teaching* (Columbus: Merrill, 1966).

which the students came. Dining, social activities, sports, and student government reinforced values the students brought with them to college.

The inculcation of values in the curriculum stemmed from a homogeneity of the faculty as much as from specific design. While typically the six-hour Bible requirement stressed the values inherent in the Judeo-Christian tradition, the greater reaffirmation of values came from direct, personal associations with faculty members who lived among the students in a community of concern. Their accessibility, sensitivity, and intuitive facility with non-directive techniques of faith-support provided nurture and contributed to the amazing loyalty among alumni that such institutions enjoy.

Secular Erosion

The erosion of values symptomatic of an increasingly secular society has had a profound impact upon church-related liberal arts colleges faced with the challenge of a student group less directly influenced by a strong, teaching church; less assured of parental support; more confused by the clamor for license in a peer group militant for freedom from restraint. The presence of these young people within the student population altered the values-reaffirming character which the Christian liberal arts colleges traditionally represented. It is axiomatic that one can only reaffirm that which has previously been affirmed. The alternative has been either to relax regulations, requirements, and distinctions, or to devise a new strategy to meet the challenges posed by the contemporary situation.

Lamentably, many colleges have demonstrated less capability to devise a new strategy than a willingness to compromise their prior mission. In the mid-1970s, Earl J. McGrath described this situation. "As far as the youth of this country seeking an institution in which religion constitutes a genuine element in the total educational experience is concerned, they are. . . likely to be denied this opportunity. . . by the [institution's] abandonment of religiously related goals and practices. . . ."[5] He urges the church-related liberal arts colleges to adhere to their own special mission and services and to reshape their policies and programs to assist the citizenry in dealing with the enormous problems faced in public and private life. "The liberal arts

---

[5]Earl J. McGrath, *Values, Liberal Education, and National Destiny* (Indianapolis: Lilly Endowment, 1975), p. 4.

college more than any other institution ought to provide the forum for enlightened discussion of...questions...about the character and quality of American life [which] boil down to *value* questions."[6]

McGrath's voice was one of many raised to protest the loss of distinctions among institutions whose differentiation in the past was not limited to the nature of funding and support. C. Robert Pace in one of the studies in the Carnegie Commission series entitled *The Demise of Diversity?*[7] warned of a steady trend toward sameness among formerly quite varied institutions. To allow one model for all higher education to become dominant would raise serious questions about the necessity for continuing privately-supported independent higher education. Only those institutions whose financial resources and support were considerable could afford to follow the lead of large state-supported universities, if indeed that should be deemed desirable.

Efforts to Expand Emphasis on Values

An institutional reaffirmation seemed in order. If the mission of reaffirming values seemed threatened by the loss of prior experiences on the part of the students coming to Christian colleges which had fostered the acceptance and development of values, then the institutions could espouse the third approach to values in the curriculum: *values expansion*. It is nearer reality to suggest that such institutions found themselves faced with a challenge to address value-laden issues or to raise value questions from all three perspectives, but particularly from the reaffirmation or rekindling of values already accepted and the expansion or further development of values through the educational programs of the colleges.

Curriculum Revision

The need for a study of the general education program seems to be a widely recognized phenomenon. As someone has observed, we seem to be in a time when the only institutions which aren't presently revising their curriculum or do not anticipate such studies are those which have just

[6]McGrath, p. 11.

[7]C. Robert Pace, *The Demise of Diversity? A Comparative Profile of Eight Types of Institutions* (Berkeley: The Carnegie Commission on Higher Education, 1974).

completed curriculum reform. Notable among those who have constructed innovative approaches to general education are a number of institutions which have sought to address the need among contemporary college students to deal with value issues. For the purposes of the paper I shall examine only two whose programs represent values-oriented general education, St. Olaf College and Louisiana College.

St. Olaf Experiment

St. Olaf College, Northfield, Minnesota, implemented a Values Program in 1975 after a successful pilot program in the prior academic year. Citing the traditional educational goals of the college as development of the intellect, the emotions and will in the context of Christian principles and the liberal arts, St. Olaf College proposed a "values-centered education as a contemporary affirmation of those objectives." The student would be challenged to understand through serious scholarly inquiry and to think critically and analytically "about the value-laden issues that confront him/her—but also, inevitably and as part of the same process, to face and to decide upon his/her own position."

Through "educational environments" that will demand both serious academic preparation and personal engagement, St. Olaf seeks to accomplish its broader objective through five goals:

"We seek to develop

(1)   an awareness of values
(2)   a capacity for the clarification and analysis of values
(3)   an understanding of the scope and limits of human choices
(4)   skill in defining issues in the context of crucial contemporary problems
(5)   an enhanced scope for self-conscious and responsible decision-making."

Values courses, interdisciplinary programs, values perspectives for majors, values semester-programs and values-focused interim term courses are among the approaches adopted by St. Olaf for this pervasive thrust in their curriculum. Wisely, the college gave particular attention to the preparation of faculty for their work in this program through workshops prior to the beginning of each academic year and through similar means. Provision was developed for evaluation of the program, as well.[8]

Louisiana College Program

Louisiana College, a liberal arts college affiliated with the Louisiana Baptist Convention, developed its Value-Centered Central Curriculum over a four-year period of study which concluded in 1977 with the implementation of the new general education program. The process of reform began in faculty discussions held in 1973 following the appointment of a new academic dean. The college had completed a study of its mission statement in connection with its accreditation self-study in 1971. The faculty felt that the purpose statement should set the parameters for a needed re-evaluation of the general education program. A committee addressed the specification of learning outcomes desired for the "ideal" Louisiana College graduate. After the faculty approved this committee report, a task force representing all elements of the college community began its study of the program through which these objectives could be attained. This study shaped the Louisiana College Central Curriculum subsequently adopted by the faculty and approved by the board of trustees.

The designation of the general education program as the Central Curriculum emphasizes its place in the college. It is principal, dominant. It constitutes that from which other emphases proceed or upon which they depend. The pervasive philosophy of the curriculum supports the apprehension of human values derived from an enlightened world view consonant with the Christian faith. To contribute to a life oriented toward values, based on knowledge, and characterized by the acquisition of skills, the college constructed interdisciplinary approaches to the tasks of teaching and learning.

Among the interdisciplinary courses are the freshman level *Faith and Human Values*, an introduction to religious experience in its relation to human existence and the need for meaning in life; the junior option, *The*

---

[8]McGrath, pp. 41-44. See also David Wee, "Values in the American College," *Forum for Liberal Education*, March, 1978, pp. 1-3; and Gary H. Quehl, ed., *Developing the College Curriculum: A Handbook for Faculty and Administrators* (Washington: Council for the Advancement of Small Colleges, 1977), pp. 233-235.

Arts and Human Values or *Science and Human Values*; and the senior capstone course, *Contemporary Society and Christian Values*. The faculty intended a cumulative effect to be derived from the sequence of values courses. While they eschewed any attempt to indoctrinate or dictate a student's apprehension of a Christian lifestyle, the expectation was that the process of discovery would facilitate the acknowledgment of the primacy of Christian values to the good life.

Value-laden issues would naturally be raised in other courses of the Central Curriculum, particularly *Biblical Perspectives* (a survey of biblical doctrine and ethics), *Language and Culture*, and *Literary Perspectives*, and in those of the *Inquiry*, Louisiana College's innovative, experiential term.[9]

To Each Institution Its Own Model

The experience at Louisiana College parallels those at other institutions where curriculum reform, giving a new shape to the general education program, has occurred. Such studies require a college or university to ask significant questions about purpose, about the centrality of faith, and about the roles of biblical studies, language, natural sciences and mathematics, the social sciences and physical education, indeed all components of the present and proposed program, in accomplishing the institution's basic and essential purpose. Curriculum study affords the opportunity for a re-examination of resources—both fiscal and personal—and their wisest use.

Investigating current approaches to an integrative thrust for its general education program may lead an institution to consider a values-centered curricular model. Landrum Bolling supports this approach in his description of the church-related college as the seed-bed and the nourishing ground for the development of moral, ethical, and spiritual values. He states, "The mission to which the church college is called. . . above everything else is the reaffirmation of those values and those purposes of life that transcend our human existence and link us to divine purposes that will outlive us."[10]

---

[9] *Louisiana College Catalogue* 1979-81, pp. 35, 74-77.

[10] Landrum R. Bolling, "Seedbed for Moral and Spiritual Values," *The Southern Baptist Educator*, XLII (No. 3, 1978), 12.

Values Emphasis A Church-Related College Distinctive

Speaking to the National Congress on Church-Related Colleges and Universities in February, 1980, the first appointee to the Office of United States Secretary of Education, Shirley M. Hufstedler, expressed a similar assessment of the distinctions of such institutions. "Your colleges," she stated, "are valuable not simply because they have stood so long against the pressures of time, but because the ideas they have stood for—and stand for—are worth preserving. First among these is a focus on human and spiritual values." After citing the growing secular academic spirit of the publicly-supported universities, which has weakened the study there of morality and faith, the Secretary observed, "In an age when technology magnifies the consequences of individual and collective actions, the need to consider questions of morality has never been greater. While justice and harmony remain elusive, who can question the need to examine and re-examine our relationship with God and with one another? The colleges that sustain such study are just as precious, just as irreplaceable, as those that sustain basic research in the physical sciences—perhaps, in the long run, even more so."[11]

Bolling reminds us that Whitehead once wrote that any true education is fundamentally religious education. Phillip Phenix, professor of philosophy of education at Columbia University, wrote ". . .effective education has always been values-oriented, and always will be, almost by definition. Instruction that interests and moves students toward worthy goals is by that very fact 'value-able,' as I see it."[12] Both are correct. Serious consideration of ultimate questions about God, about man, about truth and about the created order in which our relationships are formed are inherently spiritual and intellectual, religious and instructive. Value-centered teaching is a pathway along which we will not lose sight of these principles. A consideration of value-laden issues as a unifying thrust for a general education program can infuse the whole curriculum with new vigor. The implementation of such a curricular model in a Christian college may point our students to Milton's "true virtue, which being united to the heavenly grace of faith, makes up the highest perfection."

[11]Shirley M. Hufstedler, Secretary of Education, "Remarks to the National Congress on Church-Related Colleges and Universities," (Washington, D.C., 2 February, 1980), pp. 8-9.

[12]Howard Kirksey, "A Value-Centered Central Curriculum," *The Southern Baptist Educator*, XLII, (No. 5, 1978), 12.

X. New Pathways

Role of the Church-Related College in Regaining a Sense of National Purpose

Fred E. Harris

T he national malaise from which we are suffering is often attributed to unstable political forces. It must be so! We find increasing numbers of persons registering as independents rather than as members of either major political party. Every four years we revive, although somewhat more weakly in recent decades, the hope that "this time" we really have the right man as president. Special interest political groups focus maximum instant pressure with panzer-like efficiency on a single issue out of context with other issues, thus distorting the deliberative legislative process. And statutory law focuses on issues which go through a media blitz, cycle of "special interest" birth, unending attacks through increasingly overloaded courts, development of mechanisms for by-passing, evading or ignoring it and, finally, amendment or replacement or even nonenforcement.

Some persons would fault the judicial system, linking the system to current malaise. In recent years the courts have performed amazing feats, including determining the exact month when a fetus becomes a human being, concluding that providing books to parochial schools violates the separation of church and state while providing films does not do so, giving tenure to faculty members over the objections of the college, and redrawing political boundary lines.

Of course the government is not totally and probably not even largely ineffective. Yet its litany of lurching performances engenders a strong sense of doubt, not necessarily about integrity or purpose but about ability and even about balance.

When the cynicism engendered by actions of "the government" is combined with the narcissism of the contemporary American, a third force is created: reduction in sense of national purpose.

The phenomenon has paralleled some brilliant successes: the concept of person has been made more noble through a series of laws, notably the Civil Rights Act and the Social Security laws. Constitutional crises have been mastered with considerable confidence in the process.

But the matter of national purpose does not rest. Almost with relief some persons "welcomed" the Ayatollah who "brought us together again"!

No. Something is not right. Ultimately the government is the people. Politicians do not become corrupt or incompetent upon going to the state house or to Washington; they were actively or potentially corrupt or incompetent when they were elected.

While we saw universities deteriorate or lose purpose during the student rebellions, while we can understand that the judgments of the courts are flawed because we ask them to solve too many of the wrong kinds of problems, and while we know that the presidency has been exploited by many selfish groups and misused for years, we forget that our rate of change is so great that it causes us to use government mechanisms, agencies, laws and persons like "throw-aways." We use institutions like Kleenex. They have no intrinsic value, only uses. The exploitative attitude toward government and its institutions is the other side of the coin of government's exploitation and manipulation of its subjects. But the modest tyranny we know does not arise within government; it moves from us to others through government.

And we have a new day. Never before has this unusual combination of circumstances existed. The people are exploitative. Thus government that cannot afford politically narcissistic persons instant gratification of their needs and wishes is mocked and ridiculed. Political satire degenerates into political obscenity. The government is vilified, not because it isn't effective but because it isn't effective enough. We ask of the government that which we will not ask of ourselves, but there is an illusion: we really ask it of ourselves because we are the government.

In much the way that C. S. Lewis argued in *The Abolition of Man* that our attempts to subdue and control nature were predictions of our sure subjugation by nature, our manipulation of government for purposes of exploitation of others is ultimately exploitation of ourselves.

Assessing The Options of the Church-Related Colleges

The ebbing of national purpose is the ebbing of personal purpose and many apparent solutions to moral issues lack moral depth or even moral justification.

Given an uninspiring performance by government in its attempt to respond to or manage our basically exploitative behavior, what can the church-related college do to help renew our sense of national purpose?

First let us examine things church-related higher education should *not* do:

1. It should not enter the political arena alone. Once in that arena, the colleges would be seen and treated as political entities and would, in time, be forced to resort, more and more, to political devices. The dominance of political behavior is not the essential problem, however. The essential fact is that church-related colleges are not political entities. They are a *Third Force*, neither exclusively church nor exclusively state. Only when this identity, growing out of mission, is fully understood can the church-related college contribute effectively to our sense of national purpose. The *Third Force* identity is essential to a properly defined national purpose.

2. The church-related colleges should not lend their voices to other professional organizations. For many years "church-related" has been considered by most national professional organizations as one characteristic, among many, of a college, instead of as *the* characteristic of such colleges. The identity of the church-related college was blurred and thus less able to state its mission to an increasingly secular listener. Church-related colleges must retain the right to speak for themselves; no other organization can represent them. Crystal clear identity is essential to a properly defined national purpose.

3. The church-related college should not allow its relationship with its sponsoring church group to become diminished. Rarely is such a relationship successfully renewed when **disrupted. The exact**

176912

arrangements of the relationship are often less important than the integrity and sincerity that characterize it. Unless both the church and the college invest heavily in the relationship, much is lost by each. Strong ties with the church are essential to a properly defined national purpose.

4.   The church-related college should not let its relationship with its sponsoring group be determined by their dollar contributions made to the college. When the focus of the relationship becomes financial, one can usually be sure that much was lost before the question of dollars arose. Relationships far more substantive than dollars are necessary for the college to have a properly defined national purpose.

5.   The church-related college should not become exclusively identified with its home region. Of course such colleges are communities within communities, but they are also a part of a great national fraternity. They must accept the obligations of this relationship. A view of national mission is essential to properly defined national purposes.

In summary, church-related colleges should (a) avoid political identity, (b) let no group except its own speak for the church-related college, (c) maintain and strengthen church ties, (d) avoid an excessive dollar focus in relationship with sponsoring church, and (e) cooperate with and aid other such colleges maintaining a national view. These injunctions are meant to preserve and promote the church-related colleges as viable instruments in renewing national purpose.

The Task and the Problem of Self-Image

Before noting the positive steps that should be taken by church-related colleges to help renew our sense of national purpose, a side trip to the psychiatrist's office is recommended. The matter of self-image requires attention. No contributions of significance can be made unless the trustees, faculty members and administrators of colleges *know* they have something to contribute. They all need to recall these important facts:

1.   Church-related colleges are not merely vestiges of a noble past, now largely ineffective because of the nature of the host society. In mission, they can play an essential moderating role in a society that often finds itself in threatening disarray.

2.   Church colleges are a great national treasure. Their missions cannot be duplicated by any other unit in the society. They are in numbers,

strength, sense of mission and unselfish investment unique in all the world. No other nation has such treasures. Close the church-related colleges and watch the quick formation of a monolithic, semi- or largely politicized system of higher education. There has been great momentum in that direction for the past thirty years.

3. For many years, leaders in tax-supported colleges looked with trust and approval to church-related colleges as bastions of political and academic freedom for the whole of higher education. Now heavily secularized and often quite politicized, these leaders look to the state. But leaders of church-related colleges should never forget their role in sustaining politically and academically free higher education. Moving from the two small church-related colleges in Alaska, across the Bering Sea and through Asia, Southeast and Southern Asia and into all of the Middle East, it is now difficult to find politically and academically free public educational institutions.

4. Measured against investment and enrollment, no segment of higher education produces more leaders for the professions, the church, for industry and for the community.

5. Although suffering losses in a society that stresses materialism and status symbols, the liberal arts remain the motivating force in the educational philosophies of most church-related colleges. The more politically expedient vocational education and community college thrusts of the federal and state governments have seriously damaged but have not extinguished the humanizing spirit of a liberal arts education. The church-related college should reject the generic term "post-secondary education" and all of the political implications of that term. Church-related institutions are not extensions or tandem units of public secondary schools. They are properly the independent citadels of humanizing liberal learning.

When measured against the ebullient optimism of persons in the non-church-related higher education systems, the self-image of church college and university personnel clearly needs attention. These facts must be reaffirmed: (a) The church-related educational institution is not only relevant to today's search for national purpose; it is essential to that task. (b) Without the church-related college and university, the checks and balances system moderating national purpose would in large measure be left to the institutionalized secular forces. (c) The humanizing spirit of liberal learning rests uneasily in most arenas now but it is still the central focus of nearly all church-related colleges; in no other place does it now rest so appropriately.

The Helping Institutions

Colleges must be realistic about their own shortcomings, including infidelity to purpose. Some institutions of higher education in this country have failed their sponsoring churches, their country, their students, and themselves by casually accepting and teaching as dogma thought-systems in several disciplines that deserve far more critical analysis and inquiry than they have received. There is a great difference between preserving needed academic freedom and the uncritical acceptance of intellectual modes that permit or promote institutional deterioration to the point where the institution cannot defend its own existence or is indifferent to the reasons for its existence. In part, this ineptness and indifference explains why so many of the institutions that were once clearly Christian in purpose and program now assess and list themselves as "of denominational origin" or "traditionally related." The weakness is within the system. In this country, and in the Western World generally, institutions fail or fall not because of external assault but rather because of internal weakness. The institutions under consideration in this paragraph are those which in many ways have been open to all inquiry—even to the point of being intellectually uncritical—except their own Christianity. Institutions of this genre cannot make much of a contribution toward regaining a sense of national purpose; they cannot make a contribution to their own sense of purpose and often cannot identify it except in totally secular language or by referring to government "guidelines"—which largely define what the colleges are not.

But the focus is not on institutions which cannot make a contribution; their weakness is not as important as the general strength of *all* church-related colleges.

The colleges which will make the greatest contribution to the renewal of national purpose may well be those dealing effectively with concepts such as the following:

1.   The spirit of populism and egalitarianism which is quite consonant with the concept of individual freedom and development intrinsic to the Western World has led to a definition of equality inconsistent with the facts about the distribution of individual characteristics. Long fascinated by Jeffersonian democracy, we have forgotten that Jefferson pointed out two characteristics that are not equally held: virtue and talent. It is to these two essentials that church-related colleges have traditionally addressed themselves. Our church-related colleges will contribute to the restoration of national purpose as they intensify or return to their fundamental mission—the providing of leaders and followers of special quality required at all levels of society. For generations the church-related college performed this specific task well. We can make no greater contribution to the nation than continuing to do so and to do so with increasing effectiveness.

2.   Charles Fair in his devastating analysis of the current scene (*The New Nonsense*: subtitled *The End Of The Rational Consensus*) points to two fundamental changes in Western society that have altered our destiny: a) the abandonment of rational inquiry as a basic method for solving problems and b) the abandonment of belief in life after death. The former has led to the politicization of our universities; the latter has reduced the moral universe from eternity to a single lifetime. The ready use of the university by some economists, historians, sociologists, anthropologists and others as a forum for indoctrination is in part a consequence of our loss of command of rational inquiry. It is patently absurd to insist on the right of a Marxist to teach at a state university while insisting that Christian religion be taught only as an historical or social phenomenon. The moral consequences of changing the time frame of moral judgments surround and overwhelm us. Situational ethics, hedonism, narcissism and nihilism fit comfortably with the reduced moral time frame.

     The church-related college appears to have been less politicized, less affected by the abandonment of rational inquiry as *the* mode of inquiry and less affected by the change in the moral universe than other collegiate institutions. We serve best as we serve as a "safe haven" for the most essential unit of intellectual life—rational inquiry—much as the monasteries of the church preserved literacy and learning at another time. And the greater moral universe that characterized the church-related college preserves and enhances a definition of person and of God, now largely discounted by a society that appears to be seeking satiation in touch, toys and tunes.

What more could a nation ask of its church-related free educational institutions?